PUBLISHED BY
CASTLE COMMUNICATIONS PLC
BOOK DIVISION
A29 BARWELL BUSINESS PARK
LEATHERHEAD ROAD
CHESSINGTON
SURREY KT9 2NY

ISBN 1 898 141 150

C000100387

FAITH NO MORE
'From The Author'

This book gives you the first true and genuine account of *everything* that Faith No More have been through in their 11 year career. It is incomplete in the respect that the band are nowhere near the end of their career. Doubtless there will be a whole lot more to document in the years to come.

'The Real Story' is made up of original quotes from the five current band members, ex-singer Chuck Mosely and producer Matt Wallace. All were interviewed between February and September of 1993 exclusively for this book. Warren Entner and John Vasillou at WEM Management felt it best not to make any comments, as they still work with the band. There are also two transcripts in the 'Onward' section from which some material was used for magazine features, the reason for their inclusions are explained within.

Faith No More agreed to help me tell 'The Real Story', despite the fact they will receive no money from it's sales. Each band member donated some of his free time to talk about their life, and the band's history. The copy has since been checked for accuracy, but in no way has anyone from Faith No More tampered with the flavour of any portion of the text. It was a dream situation. I whole-heartedly thank Bill Gould, Mike Patton, Jim Martin, Mike Bordin and Roddy Bottum for their unflinching honesty and their ability to leave me alone once they had given me their input. I also thank them for being the most interesting band to emerge in the last decade. I thank Matt Wallace for his unique insight and vision of the band. And I thank Chuck Mosely for talking about what must be a very difficult subject for him to deal with. I hope he has good luck with his latest project, Cement. I must also thank Warren and John for their total support of my endeavours over the years, their trust, and the fact that they never once interfered with this project.

I would also like to say a big 'thank you' to Phil Scott for starting this whole ball rolling, to Laurie Pryor for wanting and believing in this book, to Sonia Bailey for helping the paperwork shuffle along, to Eugene Manzi for his help through the years, to Mary, Ann and Neil for just *being*, to Steve Stolder for helping me learn a little more about Grammar, to Lonn Friend for consistently supporting my work and to Geoff Barton for taking me in during the Summer of 1983 and sticking with me ever since. Oh, and thank you Deanna for the title!

Thanks also to Cliff Burton (RIP) for introducing me to Faith No More way back when. He may be gone but he isn't forgotten.

This is a book for people who like *truth*. There is no fabrication, and there are no lies in these pages. 'The Real Story' is for fans, both of Faith No More and rock music.

To: Deanna, the *fantastic* Zak Chirazi, Marie and Bob. One down...

6

FAITH NO MORE
'Cast Of Characters'

In a real-life 'drama' such as this, it was felt by my editor Phil Scott that a small 'cast of characters' may help indentify all of the protaganists to you. I have listed only those who have repetitive relevance to the band's story. As with all scenarios, this 'cast' is subject to change without any prior notice!!!

THE MAIN PLAYERS

Bill Gould - bass player and founder-member of Faith No More
Roddy Bottum - keyboard player and founder-member of Faith No More
Mike Bordin - drummer and founder-member of Faith No More
Jim Martin - guitarist and original member
Chuck Mosely - first FNM vocalist
Mike Patton - current FNM vocalist
Matt Wallace - the first, and only, producer/engineer FNM have ever worked with.

SUPPORTING CAST MEMBER

Cliff Burton - Metallica's bassist through their first three albums and instrumental friend of both Bordin and Martin's. Sadly died in a bus accident in 1986.

Mike 'The Man' Morris - frontman/guitar-player in Faith No Man
Wade Worthington - Keyboard player in Faith No Man

Gerry and Olga Gerrard - FNM's first managers

Ruth Schwarz - founder of Mordam Records, who released FNM's first album 'We Care A Lot'.

'Ghandi' Joe - semi-legendary FNM roadie in the early days

Anna Stadtman - A&R lady at Slash who signed FNM

Bob Biggs - Slash Records president

Warren Entner/John Vassilou - FNM's management team

Lenny Waronker - President of Warner Bros Records

FAITH NO MORE
'The Real Story'

1992/93

FAITH NO More can be a shocking affair. In Brixton late last year, during a 3 night 'Angel Dust Tour' stint at the cavernous Academy, Mike Patton took a tennis shoe, got his dick out, pissed in it, screamed and drank with unnerving enthusiasm. This was after he had munched upon a tampon that was lying on the stage somewhere, left as a 'snack' by support act L7. This was after he had hurled and thrown himself against the hard wooden stage repeatedly without respite for a good 45 minutes. This was after he'd leapt and jumped like a salmon, except there was no water to cushion his fall, just his legs. Patton's shins developed a condition, 'shin splints' or whatever, and he was told to slow down a bit, take it easy. He can't. How can you control what you don't know? A few years ago Patton was a rural college boy, happily bounding around with his pals from childhood band Mr Bungle, alcohol and care free, never knowing that four years later he'd drink his own piss from a tennis shoe in front of 4000 people with confused BOREDOM screaming through his head. Patton is clueless as to why he does these things, writing it off on boredom and the ever-revolving wheel of touring that makes him 'feel like a mouse chasing cheese'. Worst of all, there is no 'off' switch in sight...

BILL GOULD AND RODDY BOTTUM

Bill Gould and Roddy Bottum have been friends pretty much all their lives. Both lived a mile from each other in Hancock Park, an affluent part of Hollywood, where celebrities were as common as concrete. Gould's father was a successful high-powered lawyer, Bottum's the same. Both went to affluent schools. Both had a strong interest in music from an early age. Neither was particularly enamoured with their comfortable surroundings.

"I learned to play bass because Roddy could play piano, his Mom used to make him practice for two hours in the mornings, and a friend of ours had drums and we got some guitars," remembers Gould.
"We used to ride our bicycles around, we went to the same Grammar School, St. Brendan's Catholic School and it seemed pretty natural for us to form a band. My lot was bass and I got lessons, which nobody else did."

In every sense the phrase implies, theirs was a typical, moneyed Hollywood upbringing.
"I knew a lot of kids who came from celebrity families and I'd end up going out onto [film] sets and whatever, seeing how things were made. So I saw a lotta that shit first hand. But if you grow up in LA, the chances are you're gonna know someone from a celebrity background. Ralph Bacchi the animation guy was close by and Roddy used to baby-sit Rosanna Arquette's family. The thing is, when you live in LA you're always going to know somebody. It's an entertainment city so there's all that shit..."

"Most of our childhood was spent throwing things at people from high buildings," laughs Bottum, "I think we've carried a little of that with us right through to this day, that throwing of

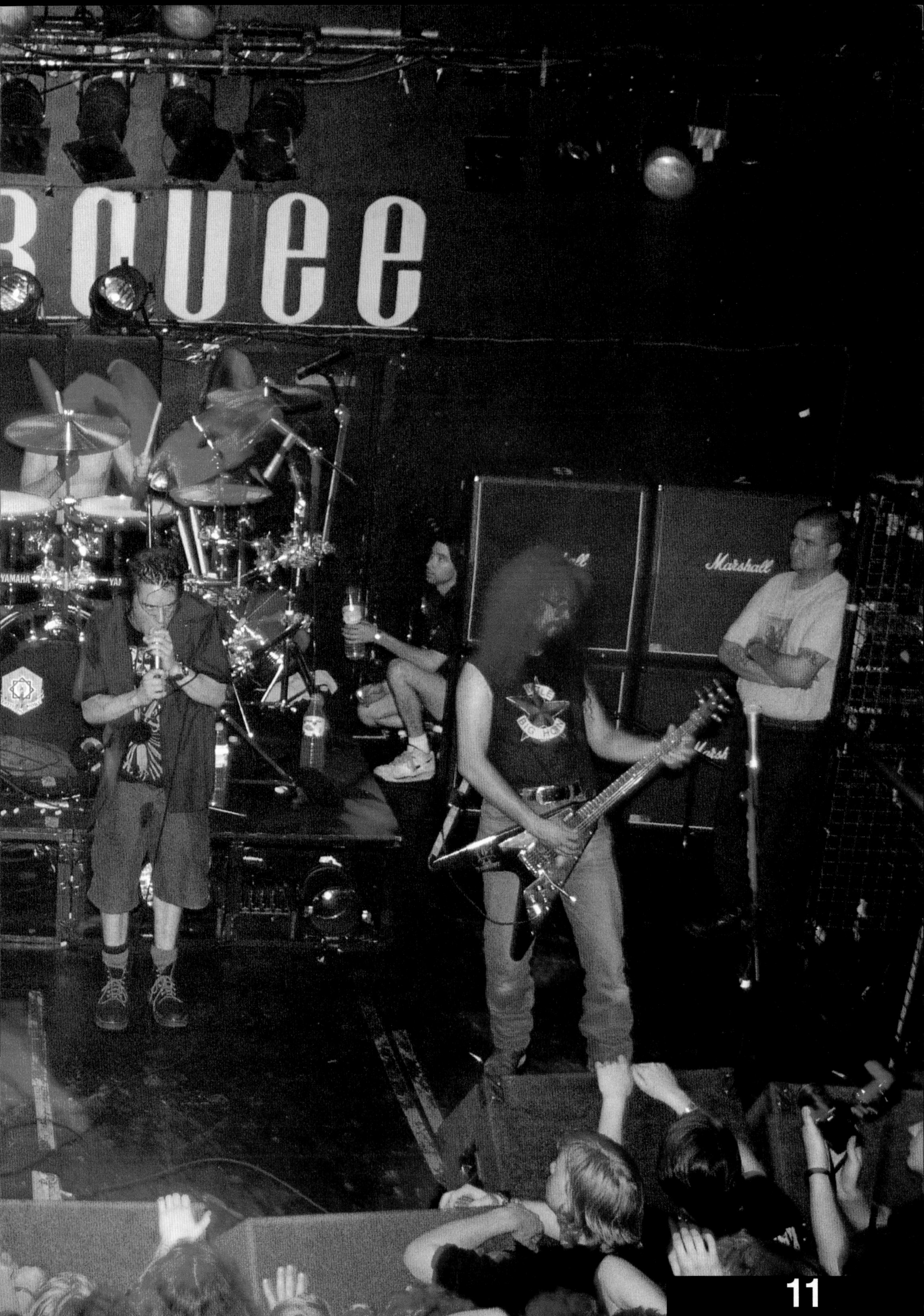
Marshall

stuff at people from high places. They can't get you from up there, you're far away, they become good targets. Prank phone calls were pretty big, and everything we used to do follows that 'high building' principle. Basically, we were just real trouble makers.

"Our neighbourhood was pretty sterile, very Hollywood. In some instances it was an exciting place and in others a dull one. But the chemistry of us getting together always meant mischief. We just always ended up causing trouble, climbing in trees and throwing things at cars. We used to make bomb-threat calls too. I remember this one time, we made a bomb threat when we were 10 years old and called up a Safeway supermarket near my house and told them there was a bomb in the store. Then we were so cocky, we walked up to the Safeway to see what had happened there. Of course there was chaos, the bomb squad was there, people had been evacuated from the store but we walked right up to the manager and said 'Hey what's going on?' No-one ever found out of course, no way! We were just trouble-making all the time."

Gould had a hunger for music from 13 years old. The bass lessons, friends and people he knew were all factors in spurring him on further.
"I hung out with older people, I played with bands in bars when I was 15, that was a great thing, but I guess the early punk scene was what really got me going. Roddy was with me the first time, there was this place called Larchmont Street. TIME Magazine had done a story in 1977 about punk rock, and I remember thinking how weird it seemed. So this one night we were riding our bikes, to go get some ice-cream from the store as funny as it may seem, and we went past these people with safety pins comin' out of their mouths and all dressed up. I was entranced, *these* were the people I'd been reading about. So we rode our bikes to where they were going, which was the Larchmont Hall. Hancock Park was a very community-oriented kind of place where everyone knew everyone else, and the big 'hang-out' was this street Larchmont.

"It was so weird at that time to have a punk gig at this Knights Of Columbus Hall or whatever in this neighbourhood-everybody-knows-what-you're-doing community. I still don't know why there was a punk gig there, but I got off my bike, paid my money and went in. There were these bands called The Zeros, Johnny Navotnee and The Bags. It was 1977, I was 12-13 years old and these guys could play bass about as well as I could, they were *horrible* but they were great. The people were wild, they *looked* like wild people and to a kid like me, that was hanging out with people living on the edge. I was walking around being really obnoxious, that was the way, and I took a liking to doing that. So I immediately started going to shows and getting into that whole scene."

BOTTUM: "There was this punk rocker that used to run a record store on Larchmont and that used to fascinate us. The first album I remember coming across and getting into was the Sparks record. It was this weird, quirky music that I'd never heard before. We'd harass this freaky guy from the store all the time, and I always managed to steal records from there somehow. I stole that Sparks record when I was 12 years old."

The first band Gould was ever in were called The Animated.
"One guy, the singer, was in my boy scout troop with Roddy and one guy, who was older, was our keyboard player. That was Chuck..."

As in Chuck Mosely, the first permanent Faith No More frontman/singer.
"I was about 14/15 when I started playing with them and Chuck was about 19. He'd go to all the shows, he was the experienced one, he'd take acid and I as still 'the kid', my Mom would drop me off at practice with my amp and guitar. So I gravitated towards him, kinda 'show me the ropes' thing and basically he's a nice guy so he liked having me around. He'd look out for me and he was pretty much responsible for turning me onto all the music I ended up liking. I didn't really know about music back then, I knew about Aerosmith, Kansas and the shit you could hear on the radio but I didn't know about the underground. I mean, I was a kid and my parents weren't particularly dialled into that stuff. My Dad liked Led Zeppelin, and Led Zeppelin to me will always be Catholic school, I associate the two because they were above-board, uninteresting, acceptable. They weren't sub-culture."

Bottum's distaste for traditional rockers wasn't quite as strong as Gould's rampant disgust.
"I liked Neil Young when I was in High School, and he wasn't liked very much. I mean, the whole Led Zeppelin 'dinosaur' thing wasn't anything I particularly hated but it wasn't anything I got into that much. I can understand how someone would hate it though. I mean the group of kids we used to go to High School with were really into all that stuff. Boston, Kansas, Zeppelin were all the big thing back then with everyone except us. X and The Plugz were the first bands I really got into, The Plugz were this great Chicano (Latin) threesome who played with X a lot, so I'd see them both together on the same shows. I really embraced that whole thing, and X were amazing simply because of their energy. It was all so different to what was going on at the time, until then I think I'd been very naive. I was really young, and the only musical spectrum I had had was that older stuff like Jackson Browne and Neil Young. And to think they were current at that age was pure naivety. And then to see this whole scene erupt, in our neighbourhood, in Hollywood, it was really exciting."

Like many young and restless Angelians, there was a rising feeling that barriers had to go. Before long, an explosion similar to that which hit Britain full-on in 1977 was brewing in the nicest parts of town. The glamour-glitter city was about to house an outburst of sweat, spit and anger.
GOULD: "To a young kid the whole punk thing represented ripping all that old shit down and DOING something. Some people say that was just a bunch of bullshit, but I saw it as being active, that's how it affected me. So I got in a band with Chuck, Roddy's 18 and in another scene altogether."
Even when Gould and Mosely were in The Animated together, Bottum still saw him.
"We always kinda hung out together, and even when we didn't see each other so much because The Animated did their thing at the weekends, we were always great friends. We started seeing each other a whole lot more again once we both ended up moving here for school. I moved to San Francisco primarily because I liked the film program at SF State College and I wanted to get involved in it."

The motivated young Gould had already attempted to launch a recording career by going to Europe.
"I had just been to England to try and get distribution for The Animated, I had started my own little record company. It kind of failed. I lied to the distributor, told them we were planning a UK tour just to get them to pick up the record! Every time I'd call to see how the record was doing, they'd ask me when I was coming over with the band and I kept on saying 'next month next month'. I was 18 with limited funds, so it wasn't ever going to happen. But the rest of the band weren't really motivated, Chuck wasn't motivated by much of anything. The best thing Chuck knew was how to get out of work, loaf around, drink beers, get into shows free by climbing through windows, finding the scam. He was the short-cut master. The band was hitting the wall so I just decided that I was gonna get the fuck out of town, go to school up North and start all over again."

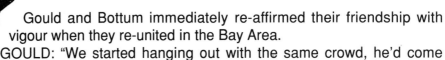

Gould and Bottum immediately re-affirmed their friendship with vigour when they re-united in the Bay Area.

GOULD: "We started hanging out with the same crowd, he'd come over to San Francisco a lot and finally he moved over here and we moved in together. And it became the same as when we were really young, throwing things at people from high buildings. So the week before school started, this was 1981, I stayed with Roddy in the dorms because he was the only guy I knew up there. I went into English and Philosophy and he was doing film but we didn't know what we wanted to do, we were looking not to work too much and get the easiest thing we could. I mean I was up in the Bay Area to be in a fuckin' band, that's what I was there for. So I stayed with Roddy and pretty much started to hang-out with him."

Berkeley, California is world famous for it's university. The campus has always attracted a wide variety of free-thinkers, activists and weirdos. It was the only town that stood a chance of being home to Faith No More's humble beginnings.

GOULD: "I went into this record store in Berkeley and saw an ad up on the wall for these guys looking for a band. These strange guys came over, one played guitar, one played keyboards and they knew a drummer. They tried me out at the same time they tried him out...the drummer was Puffy."

MIKE BORDIN

Mike Bordin, Faith No More's drummer, is one of the world's more intense people. He's a multi-dimensional character, quiet, highly strung, a touch psychotic. Perfectly suited to work with the likes of Gould and Bottum. For him, music was life.

"There was always music. I can't remember the song but it was all AM radio, from 'Hey Joe' to whatever teenie-bopper stuff you can think of. And it was so exciting to hear this stuff, I mean I'm not the sort of person who jumps up and down and screams when they're excited, I tend to sit back and say 'alriiight' and it was kinda like that. A revelation! AM radio was something that just transformed you. Sometimes you don't know what you lack or need until you get it. And all of a sudden you get it and think 'shit I'm finally whole' when you didn't even know you were half before. Even before AM radio I was dragged to the opera by my Dad, who's a big opera fan. As a gift to himself when I was born he bought season tickets to the San Francisco Opera, and he's had them since. I still have that first AM radio today, the chalk marks on it for the stations, and that thing never left my room. I remember Creedence Clearwater Revival being huge back then, and so they were my first big obsession.

"I remember them coming through, it might have been their last gig in the Bay Area at the Oakland Coliseum, and it was responsible for that first bit of trauma I had with my parents: I *had* to go to this show. I didn't go. You don't forget stuff like that. But it was a time when people like Booker T, The Isley Brothers all those guys were huge, The Staple Singers were on the radio. I know the soul songs of that era! I could remember song lyrics to any shitty song you wanna tell me about, but nothing from school or school work! I couldn't tell you who the 15th president was. I did poorly with memory stuff in school it just didn't connect. But these fucked up *stupid* songs, I could tell you how they go. Like this song 'Chikka-Boom', which is about this girl who keeps taking her clothes off in different rooms and this guy keeps chasing her. Just ridiculous, retarded songs like *that* ! I mean, I'd graffiti my text books with stupid shit like, 'this book belongs to Tony Iommi' or whatever. School never connected, music did."

Bordin suffered a family tragedy at an early age, something which perhaps contributed to the isolationist's love of music, his ultimate escape from the world.

"Honestly I don't really care to get into it, but yeah we changed family members, there was some tough shit with my folks. Maybe there's an element of truth to to the 'escape' thing, but more than that music was my identity. I was the guy in school who had the big hairdo, I was the guy who had a different Black Sabbath shirt for every day of the week, I was the guy who had posters all over my wall. I still have those too, in my house, in the basement. That is who I was, that was my trip. The only thing that happened to me was fucking-rock-music. I can't say it any plainer than that.

"I had a subscription to Circus, I had a subscription to Creem. I'd ride my bike down the record store and when records were 3 dollars a pop I'd buy $25 worth of them. I still remember the first album I bought, it was Creedence Clearwater Revival's 'Cosmos Factory'. All the guys there got to know me and they'd tip me off to this and that, had I heard any Aerosmith records. Then I developed a real problem with Black Sabbath. Once it was Creedence, Jimi Hendrix, the Rolling Stones, ELP, Deep Purple but once there was Black Sabbath that-was-it."

Quite why such a doomy band should become such an obsession is worth knowing.

"I kinda hate to even say it because it'll be an over-simplication. But in trying to explain I'll say it as the sound: incredible guitar, big heavy sound of jackboot hitting someone in the head, the incredible bass below it

"We always kinda hung out together.."

rumbling all around, all exciting and shit, the drums wild and untamed and the singing like banshee-wail screaming. They say that type of music is good for kids who feel kinda grizzly about things. It was grizzly and I dug it! Me and two other people stole a car from our friend's neighbour to see Black Sabbath in LA on the '77 tour. We also stole his gas credit card, and went to Anaheim.

"The weirdest thing is that despite all that stuff, I never really thought about playing music or drums, except for this one time. Me and Cliff Burton [a school chum from early on] were at his house, in his room, the top of the shoe-box was down with the rolling papers on it, the seeds over here and the music on. He was really into Kiss, and suddenly he said 'I wanna play bass' so I said 'I wanna play drums'. That simple! We were both about 14 years old, it was right at the beginning of the Summer. The first time we played together was on the back of this guy Kenny's porch. Cliff's parents had bought him a Rickenbacker bass which I thought was incredibly nice, his parents were the greatest, I had shitty drums, we played 'Jean Genie'. And after that, forget about it! As often as we could, as much time as we could spend. We'd jam at Jeb's barn, that was a big thing. Jeb was an East Bay guy who just liked to play, and even in his Metallica days Cliff would go and jam at Jeb's barn. Cliff and I played together for two years before Cliff heard this guy needed a bassist and drummer for his band. That was Jim Martin's band, EZ Street, and that's how we all met. Even though he was from the next town down, Hayward, we never had reason to go there before then. We went to San Francisco to see shows, Tommy Bolin, Mahogany Rush, Robin Trower, J Geils Band shows at The Winterland time but Hayward? Fuck no."

Bordin and Jim Martin's 'relationship' has been longer than either's with Faith No More. The two have never really understood or liked each other too much, but for some reason they repeatedly ended up together.

"My big point of wondering about Jim around that time was 'does he think to himself like he talks?' Even more so then than now, he used to have this 'language' that he'd talk with these guys from school, like 'yabwock', 'you're a green apple, a green asshole.' He was just a tripper. These days he seems more sedate but he was a fuckin' tripper, a huge weirdo back then. So I quit that band, I hated Jim, I fuckin' hated him, he was a total dick. I guess I was a dick too, because I couldn't take it."

Of course, Martin does remember things differently.

"At that time of course I wanted to be in a successful band. But things are muddled and you assume that it's too much to hope for so you just get on with it anyhow. So we were playing various church fairs, played a baptism once, and the Battle Of The Bands in Hayward when we started playing in this place in Berkeley called 'International Cafe'. All our friends would come along and the Greek guys who owned it would serve us booze. So we'd all drink wildly and play the tunes. When Cliff Burton joined he was about the same as us playing-wise, and he brought Puffy into the band because we needed a drummer. He had a huge afro, his hair was so huge it looked like a puffball. So we started calling him 'Puffhead' which then shortened to Puffy. Eventually, various aspects of Puffy revealed themselves along the way, and he was sacked because he was an asshole. He may say he left but either way what really is the difference? The result is the same. (He's) always talkin' shit about someone, still does now. That's why I've always hated him."

Bordin maintains the claim that he quit.

"For some reason Jim was never able to face that."

At this point Bordin must have felt his band-sharing days with Jim Martin were over. There was no contact between them and no reason to believe there ever would be again. They hated each other remember?

"Well, Jim and Cliff played together for a while and it was right after that I graduated High School, which was the same time those two hooked up. I didn't see much of Cliff for a couple of years. He had stopped playing with Jim and joined up with a band called Trauma. I was doing my little thing, Cliff his and Jim, to the best of my knowledge, was painting houses. He drove this little orange Honda in the days when guys drove Mustangs, which only emphasized to me what a fuckin' weirdo he was. But yes I wanted to lose touch with Jim, I didn't wanna talk to him, couldn't deal with it."

For Bordin, this was a time of mounting stress and anxiety which manifested itself in short, violent outbursts. He was also about to enter a strange phase of self-mutilation, cutting himself lightly on a repetitive basis.

"Right about that point I was getting really frustrated, and I'd just kick my drums over whilst we were playing. I was frustrated as hell, I couldn't express myself properly and I was shitty! I'd only been playing four or five years, and the next band I was in was this 'enlightened' Rush-style music. So I got three or four more drums, a couple of those 'twisty-style' gongs and I *still* couldn't play. We were shitty, the guitar player was a total tweek and the only show we played was two songs at our school, which were so loud that we got tossed off the stage. I had been sent away to school at that time in Menlo Park for being a bad kid. That basically meant selling pot. I don't think my folks know to this day how much pot I was selling. I had a job too, working at a toy store. Then there was this little thing about setting off a fire in the school yard, and my parents realized there was less and less control going on. I was definitely a stoner kid, my down-vest jacket, the afro.

"But this boarding school was full of these fairy [spoilt, privileged brat-types] guys, total dicks. There were some princes from the Middle East, the guy who shot King Feisal, his son was there before he got kicked out, Patty Hearst went to the college, it was a school for rich fuck-ups. Even though we weren't rich my parents wanted to do right by me, but all I cared about was music. I did exactly what as necessary to get a 'B' minus and not a bit more, and drove everybody crazy with my dorm room drum -kit. I suddenly got serious, decided that I had to stop smoking pot to get serious about my playing. Then I got interested in school, I started reading things which was all brought on by 'A Clockwork Orange' and a mellow set of English teachers. My one friend from that school was this guy Rich, he's a nut! He works at a heavy nuclear plant as a designer and he's a maniac, but he's sharp. We both hated everybody because they were a bunch of fairies."

Bordin's musical education was about to get a significant boost from the local airwaves.
"It was at that time I remember the first punk rock DJ in the Bay Area, on KSJO, it was Howie Klein. He played outcast music, The Ramones, Television, The Dictators, The Stranglers and so *that* started changing things. Instead of the ambitious, over-bloated fake progressive shit that I couldn't play anyway I started getting into the stripped down pure attitude, it really fuckin' hit. It was a new world opening up. I still loved Black Sabbath, but this school encouraged me to think for myself. From there I wanted to play even more, I wanted to continue and progress as a player. Roxy Music were another bridging point, they were a lot of things stylistically, seen as being in both worlds and that was a band I'd liked for a long time. So I was encouraged. The Dictators were a big thing, simply because they were right there between Heavy Metal and punk rock."

By this stage Bordin was playing in New Wave groups and dressing the part.
"I played in one band where I wore a Boy Scout shirt, it was fun and I was still shitty. There was one nice guy in that band, Ricky Clare, **"there was some tough shit** who had the first U2 record, the first PiL **with my folks"** album, Killing Joke. He knew his shit. I mean, me and Cliff had seen the Sex Pistols together at The Winterland [a legendary San Francisco venue since shut down] on their last stand. We went to Winterland all the time before it shut, I've got a pieces of the Winterland y'know. People should write books about THAT place, because nobody had a bad time there. It was in this shitty neighbourhood but there we were, 14 and going regularly. So we had seen that, the seed had been planted and all of a sudden I hear the first Killing Joke LP. At this point I was 16-17, these guys were in their 20's, and I was frustrating for them. So that band ended, and the guy [Clare] said he knew this person who wasn't just into Killing Joke and whatever, it was his whole life, his whole thing. I was told he was difficult to deal with, but I hooked up with him anyhow. This was 'the Man'. And there was this skinny little weirdo guy who couldn't play properly with him, Bill, a *weirdo*."

Gould too was instantly aware how different Bordin was.
"I saw that Puffy was coming from a whole other world to me and to them. Those guys were kinda older and stuffy. They wore long overcoats, looked depressing and liked Peter Gabriel and Joy Division. They acted like they were from Manchester when they were really from Castro Valley! 'The Man' Mike Morris, had The Face, Sounds and NME all over his walls; and he lived in a trailer in Castro Valley! Puffy was this total straight-above guy, kinda New Wavey. He was into the Stray Cats, had a girlfriend, a nice job at the Toy Store. I knew nothing about his Heavy Metal background, apparently those years had been his 'good' years, he had been a fuck-up as a kid and now he was making something of himself. He heard Killing Joke for the first time in 1981, Theatre Of Hate all that stuff. Their drumming styles were a bit different and he was a total rock drummer at that time, so this stuff interest-

ed him a lot. It was cool because he was learning new stuff, he saw Echo And The Bunnymen live, he tried all sorts of new things."

BORDIN: "I was pretty hyper, pretty excitable, pretty wound-up and pretty impatient. Which is a reason I grew my hair long, as an exercise in patience even though Roddy and Bill claim it was an exercise in filth. I would get very depressed very easily. I suffered huge mood swings back then. These days I feel pretty good, but back then it wasn't always so, and what I was then remains a big part of what I am now. At that time, Killing Joke and PiL were my thing, big-time, low-end driving rhythm. Bill was going to Berkeley University too, he had a funny haircut and was into The Misfits. I was turned on to The Misfits by him, I turned Cliff onto them and he turned his boys (Metallica) onto them, that's how stuff worked. I drove Bill back home one day from school and I played a Roxy Music tape. When he said 'I really like them' I knew we had common ground."

Gould and Bordin became bandmates with 'The Man'.

GOULD: "At first we were called 'Sharp Young Men' but that was just too hokey, we wanted something cryptic. So it came to be called Faith No *Man* . Wade Worthington was on keyboards and Mike Morris was the lead guy and guitar player. "

Bordin further remembers that first band being less than spectacular.

"Bill was terrible, we were all terrible together and we played for about a year in the keyboard player's garage in Castro Valley, he quit but let us carry on using the space anyway out of guilt or something. This guy, 'The Man', was very authorative. He had a vision of what he wanted and all power to him, but it was as oppressive as hell. He dumped on Bill a lot, which is one reason I think Bill doesn't like taking shit from anyone. I remember Bill and I were really into dance hall reggae at that time, and he would tell us we couldn't listen to it because it was 'irrelevant'."

Producer Matt Wallace remembers: "They were an artsy-crafty band with some Killing Joke influences - quite a unique blend of people. Mike Morris, a little older with more experience but Bill obviously knowing what he wanted, so those two clashed. Then there was Wade, who wasn't a sane person. He was a little left of centre and someone who saw things differently. But one of the beauties of his very unique perspective were his keyboard sounds; they all had a lot of noise that was part of the 'melodics' in the sound. He was very talented, and I think he helped with a lot of ideas."

GOULD: "It got kinda stifling, Wade Worthington left and we didn't know who we were gonna get at the time. Roddy was my roomate at the time and he had this cheesy little Juno Six keyboard. He was foolin' around for fun, playing and smoking pot. I knew his piano background obviously, so I asked him if he wanted to join the band. He'd never done that kinda shit before, been in bands or anything."

"Musically the hook-up for me had started when my Mom got me piano lessons," recalls Bottum, "we'd play a lot together. She was a genius though she's not professional. She's got perfect pitch, she can play any song she hears in any key. My Mom and I always had a close relationship, I remember hearing her play when I was a kid. Before I moved to San Francisco, I'd still only played acoustic piano. Then I progressed to playing electronic keyboards, and it suddenly struck me that I could play keyboards in a band. I remember Faith No Man having a keyboard player themselves, which really opened my eyes too. A lot of stuff was coming from Britain back then, it was the days of Ultravox and even Killing Joke had a keyboard, so suddenly it was a legitimate instrument that I'd never really considered before. So I started pursuing using a keyboard in the band sense, and then Billy's keyboard player quit and I joined them."

Bottum's perception of Bordin on those early meetings was just as defined.
"He was absolutely nuts, full of energy, bouncing off walls, psychotic. I think what sums him up then was that he was this insane driver just absolutely out of his mind, tailgating, going fast. Everything was a near accident for him, he was just out of his mind and I think he was doing a lot of speed too which just added to this insanity. But an incredible drummer, which was the main and obvious thing, everyone said it and everyone knew it. At that point his personality was really interesting to me, nothing he did or said was offensive it was kinda exciting. He was just this wild kid. I mean we were all a little wilder back then."

Worthington's last show was also Bottum's first, at a dive club in San Francisco's Tenderloin district called The Sound Of Music. Worthington finished the first half of the set and Bottum took on the second. It was a smooth transition.

"At first we were called 'Sharp Young Men' but that was just too hokey, we wanted something cryptic. So it came to be called Faith No *Man*..."

GOULD: "Roddy fitted in perfectly, and it was only a short matter of time before we realized we couldn't stand the singer. Me, Puffy and Roddy were getting along really well, were around he same age and had a lot in common. So one day we all 'quit' the band, which is kinda a polite way of kicking out the singer. We had called him 'The Man' because he was older, bossier, he wanted me to dress as some New Romantic or some shit like that. So finally we just told him to fuck off, yet he'd managed to brainwash us into believing that we couldn't write songs. So we were afraid that we might've needed him. That made firing him a big stab in the dark. But then we started coming up with all this cool stuff, where we pretty much threw caution to the wind and said 'if we can't come up with good stuff what the fuck we'll have a good time trying?' That's how we came up with our basic first sound, and it was a liberating kind of thing. We didn't give a fuck if we never got a record deal, we didn't give a fuck about anything. We were just playing music we couldn't play with anyone else."

BOTTUM: "It was really Mike Morris' band, and he was a terrorist. I am aware that I'm the one who pretty much saw that they left him, if I hadn't joined they'd probably have stuck with him a lot longer. The combination of the three of us was a lot stronger than just them. We were hanging out around each other a lot, talking amongst ourselves, preparing to oust that guy."

BORDIN: "One thing led to another and we both realized that 'The Man' was a slave-driver, a bit of a dick. The keyboard player quit, Roddy came in and he isn't the type to be browbeaten by anyone. We liked playing with each other, there was something going on and it didn't have to *be* anything. For the first time it wasn't bad rock, it wasn't bad progressive, it was bad whatever! It was bad 'everything'. Right around that time I started studying with the African dude at Berkeley. We all knew we had to quit because this guy was unbearable, so

we did and ended up playing together."

The Faith No Man line-up did one single, 'Song Of Liberty', which was produced by one Matthew Wallace, the man who was to become Faith No More's producer and '6th member'.

MATT WALLACE

Born in Tulsa, Oklahoma, Matt Wallace spent from ages 3 to 15 travelling with his Dad, who was a pilot. The formative years of Wallace's life were spent in a Japanese town called Fussa just outside Tokyo, where he got switched onto electronics through the Japanese pre-scouts (Weblows). By the age of 13 he'd already developed a primitive 'noise-reducer'.

Wallace grew up listening to the likes of Grand Funk Railroad, Deep Purple and Black Sabbath. He also tinkered in bands himself, learning proficiency on every standard instrument. By the time his parents moved back to Northern California in the East Bay town of Orinda, he'd decided to build a small studio in his parent's garage. They invested in his scheme and before he knew it, Wallace was in local band demand and happy to get into production. At the time he was also going to Berkeley University to study being an English teacher.

"It became 'hip' for SF punk bands to come out and record in 'Matt's garage in suburbia'," he cheerfully recounts, "and I first met William Gould even before the Faith No Man days. There was a band called Your First Born from UC Berkeley, they went to record up in the studio and they brought along this young upstart pain-in-the-ass Bill Gould, who I guess was their mentor/friend/ producer/whatever. So we're driving up to the studio along this windy suburban road and Bill Gould is flipping off EVERYONE, saying 'fuck you.' I said to him 'Bill please be cool, we have to pull into my parents garage shortly.' I think Bill has always been the muck-raker-hellraiser. He was very much against the grain, was definitely intelligent and had a smart mouth. I think he liked to challenge people and get their blood going. So a few months later Bill called and asked me if I wanted to record this band Sharp Young Men, which I did. We did their first three-song demo and they recorded the 'Song Of Liberty' single on Ministry Of Propaganda Records, which was Mike Morris' idea. The 'A' side had Adolph Hitler in a tu-tu."

"It became 'hip'.."

While most bands were trying to be someone else, the range and variety of Faith No Man's influences rendered them totally unique. Try throwing Basement 5, Magazine, The Stranglers, Joy Division, the Sex Pistols, The Damned, Discharge, The Misfits and some African drum music into a pot and developing a 'genre'; it won't happen. Free to pursue their own 'direction', the band became increasingly bizarre. With 'The Man' ousted, a new name was necessary. A long-time friend of Gould, Will Carpmill, suggested that they call themselves 'Faith No *More*' seeing as 'the man' was essentially no more. It stuck. In 1981 Faith No More was finally born, players in place but without a singer.

Many musicians have championed the use of marijuana in their work. Bill Gould, Roddy Bottum and Mike Bordin were no exceptions.

GOULD: "We were really into smoking pot, and this sound was new to us, it was cool. We didn't have a singer and so we decided that we wouldn't necessarily have one. We made the decision to play every show with a different singer and record each gig. We still have a catalogue of tapes from then, mostly with different songs on them. It was something I picked up from the Throbbing Gristle/Psychic TV era, where they used to document every show, and I admired that. So our first gig was with a guitarist Jake from this band Crucifix and our first singer was called Joe Pye from the band Pop-O-Pies. We played with them a few times. They used to play 'Truckin' over and over again, get shit thrown at them, a very annoying band overall. Sometimes it'd be one song, one note over and over again, and the ashtrays would come flying at your head, people *begging* you to change the chord, and you'd just play it over and over again. He lasted for one show! Then we had this guy Walter who was a friend of ours: 'Two pints of wine, six parts of gin, put me in the condition I am in' that's one of his lyrics. 'Drinking like a fish, smoking like a dragon, we'll soon be riding the paddywaggon,' there's more!"

BORDIN: "We wanted to be able to smoke a reefer and jam for a half-hour, the *same* thing, until it became psychotic. The song 'Zombie Eaters', the start of that song was the first thing we ever jammed as Faith No More, except we jammed it for thirty minutes before stopping. At that time we moved into this rehearsal space where people like DRI, The Dicks, Frightwig and other ruling underground punk bands were playing. That was when we came into our own as in me, Bill and Roddy. I was taking that class on (African) percussion with jocks and meatheads, real idiots, but the teacher CK was heavy. Couldn't play conventional drums to save his life, but can play seven different hand drums and then sing different patterns against all the different rhythms he's playing. Then there was PiL with their big booming bass lines of dub reggae, the rawness of Killing Joke and how they approached rhythm, all of that stuff was going on and it was inspirational. No-one was saying what you *needed* to have or do, so just taking in those different aspects was giving me the various tools I needed to make things work for my playing. It all somehow worked, and it was fun to play. I don't think it was fun to listen to because we still sucked, but we were enjoying it. From there we experimented with all these singers but it didn't matter, it didn't make any difference. We wanted to get somewhere that was a million miles away, and we decided to start taking the appropriate steps."

1983

The mix-and-match era continued in earnest. When Gould wasn't wearing a dress onstage, he was indulging himself in psychotic trance-like bass loops with a variety of different singers wailing over it all.

GOULD: "Paula Fraser sang and played guitar for a show, she was a great singer from a local underground band Frightwig. We were constantly going through guitarists and singers all the time, but it was fine because we just kept on trying new stuff and had these tapes done. People started coming to our shows and they (the shows) became kinda creepy. We'd burn a lot of inscence, smoke a lot of pot and people would get into what we were doing even though we really didn't want to be 'a band' as such. We were much more into the assault mode. It started becoming like music, and the last fuckin' thing we wanted to be was a rock band! We really wanted to be aggressive though, to make this ambient music that was totally aggressive. This girl Courtney came along, she saw us play and made the huge pitch about knowing what we wanted and being able to do it. She stayed for about 3 or 4 shows,

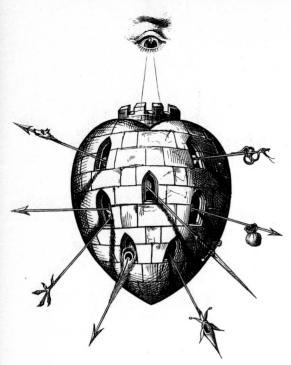

and she was good because she was as annoying as hell and *really* aggressive. But at that time she couldn't sing too well, and she had a lot of personal problems, so she had to leave the band."

The 'Courtney' in question is none other than the infamous Courtney Love, who has since steered her band Hole to a record deal with Geffen, and who is married to Nirvana's Kurt Cobain. She and Bottum remain friends to this day, the two having had a few wild dates back in those early days.

GOULD: "It got to this point where things were just too much. Courtney's not the sort of person you could be an equal with in a bands, she's got to lead and tell people what's what. She was the dictator, and in our band things were democratic. Which all meant she had to fuck off. So we headed down to LA, still without a singer."

Once in LA, the band realized that perhaps an old friend of Gould's was worth checking out. Chuck Mosely couldn't sing a blind note but no-one seemed to care so outrageous and 'spazz-energized' were his stage performances.

"I just told him to have a few beers and get out there, yell whatever the hell he wanted," laughs Gould, "we trusted his judgement and he went nuts, screamed his lungs out, went absolutely ape-shit which was great because we wanted someone to just put out like that."

BORDIN: "I remember what Bill said when we got Chuck in the first place. He said 'Let's get this guy Chuck and fuck singers, let's just leave him in there, he doesn't give a fuck, he'll be easy to get on with.' Chuck was never a singer, he didn't give a fuck and that's all we wanted. We didn't want a singer, we didn't want a Steven Tyler. We probably would've dealt with Steve Jones better, because he had attitude. We were just happy to have someone who would talk over our trance-like music."

Bottum was fully aware of Chuck from the LA days.

"I'd known him in Los Angeles when he was in Billy's band. The whole thing with Chuck was that it started out a certain way and never really changed. He lived in LA, we lived in San Francisco. We'd send him tapes of what we were doing and he'd learn from the tapes, come up for the shows and arrive 20 minutes before we'd go on. Then he'd leave the next morning. It was always like that. We were never really a 'band', this close-knit group of people that talked together, it was always this thing where we were the people up here doing most of the work, setting up the shows, writing the music, making the tapes, getting the contacts. But he was very unique, I don't think there was ever anyone who got away with stuff like him. His vocal stretch wasn't much and the way I see it he doesn't have a whole lot going for him. But he can get away with it because he has this unique charm. He has a simplicity that somehow works for him."

CHUCK MOSELY

Born in Hollywood, California, Mosely was adopted at one year old by his parents from a Children's Home society. Growing up in South Central LA and Venice, he was enrolled in piano lessons from the ages four to thirteen by his family.

"They say that when Batman came out I wanted to play it. I don't really remember that too well, but they interpreted it as getting me a piano and having me take lessons for the next 10 years. I had to, arrgggh! I remember the first Beatles record clearly, I remember hearing about The Beatles, The Beatles, The Beatles and then I finally *heard* them. I loved that first record, then I got their second and so on. I also had Alvin And The Chipmonks and The Supremes, because my sister who took care of me was really into Motown music. I liked listening to lots of different stuff."

It was almost pre-destined that Mosely would become a musician.
"My Mom played piano and my Dad played harmonica, drums and sang. So it was like being in a family of plumbers. After dinner, we'd all get around to playing things. My Mom never really performed for anybody though, she'd just take the lessons."
There was to be an unpleasant early memory from these get-togethers.
"As soon as I started taking lessons, I had to play for everybody. People would come into the house and it would be, 'Play on the piano for them,' and I really hated that shit, that's one thing I really remember hating along with practice. I didn't like being made to do it. If there was a piano around I'd just start playing it, but when people would start comin' around and watching me, when I'd stop for a moment to think about something, they'd say 'don't stop carry on' and I'd get freaked out and not play at all. I dunno, I guess I was just shy. I do much better work when I'm not being scrutinized. I've never been able to work at a job where I was near my boss.

"I actually only started singing with them because they needed someone for a couple of shows and we both thought it'd be cool."

I did that one time and I got fired, so from then on I did delivery jobs where I was by myself all the time. I work better when I'm left alone and I can still feel I'm part of the machine. And when I first started singin' with them guys, I wasn't a singer. I'd just gotten used to playing piano!"

Mosely remembers first meeting Gould in those early days on Larchmont Boulevard and laughs at the thought of him being a 'mentor' figure.
"It's funny because when we first started hangin' out, Billy and me, I hadn't been to that many punk rock shows because nobody else would go. I went to the ones I could get to and ended up at, but my friend who I used to go to shows like that with moved to England. I was 17-18 and Billy was getting into all that shit too, so we'd go to shows together, The Germs, whoever was playing. And then in The Animated we were the best buddies, because we were the only ones who hung out every night and went out."

Mosely chuckles at the memory of becoming Faith No More's frontman. The process was far from orthodox.
"I never really auditioned for them, it was just that they had Courtney. When Billy moved to Berkeley and quit The Animated we kept in touch, and when he was down in LA he'd bring tapes around of what he was doing and stuff. So I was following their progress from the Sharp Young Man stage. I actually only started singing with them because they needed someone for a couple of shows and we both thought it'd be cool."

The band invited Mosely on-board, and with a guitarist called Mark Bowen not really working out, they turned to Cliff Burton for advice.
GOULD: "We went to San Francisco in early '84 and invited Chuck to join up. We did three or four shows like that, with the old guitarist, and it just wasn't working out. Metallica were

just starting to happen at the time and Puffy still kept in close contact with Cliff.

Burton was a musical genius and someone who's opinion Bordin respected on all matters. He reminded Bordin of Martin, saying they should try him out. Bordin brought the suggestion back to the band and everyone was in agreement.

GOULD: "Puffy used to tell me about when he was in a band with Jim before us. He said he hated him, that the guy was a motherfucker, that he could go fuck himself *but* maybe he'd got better and was cooler now!"

"We had this oath that every show we did would be different songs with a different singer and hopefully a different guitar player."

BORDIN: "It was all because of Cliff. We started talking again, hangin' out and whatever. And he told us that Jim needed a gig. He told us Jim was weird, we were weird, give him a gig and be weird together. I immediately said it again, that I thought Jim was a fucking dick, a pain in the ass. But we needed a metal-ish guitar player, someone who was very aggressive to help us achieve the power we were looking for. We wanted to be like a mud-slide, a lava flow THAT sort of power. So he suggested we try it with Jim and we did. And I hope Jim would be the first to say it, but he had absolutely no clue what the fuck we were doing. Though he did find it interesting. I mean he was from Hayward for God's sake! We were listening to Black Flag, Throbbing Gristle, PiL, Echo And The Bunnymen and here's this metal dinosaur who's into Floyd, Zeppelin and so on. But that was his thing and good for him.

"This was all before Metallica made their first album and bridged the gap between punk and metal. Then there was Black Flag, who were always very heavy. I can't emphasize that enough, extremely heavy especially live. Some of their early live shows with Henry Rollins, man, you saw them and you knew what it was like to touch the sun! It was all about energy and strength, burning two holes in the wall with your eyes through sheer strength. And that's what we tried to do, that's what we'll always try to do. That's this band's foundation."

GOULD: "So just to fuck around, me, Puffy, Cliff and Jim got this one-off band together called The Chickenfuckers. We got as drunk and wasted as we could and opened for 45 Grave at the Mabuhay Gardens in San Francisco. I was singing and smoked two joints, Puffy's kick drum had a picture of a chicken with a dick down it's throat and a pentagram, which was how 'seriously' we took things. Jim said he wanted to play with us, and it was really weird at first. He was coming from Michael Schenker and all that shit, everything I completely detested. Hating isn't even the word, I had based my whole life against it. It was almost a religious thing. He wanted to play guitar solos but we beat him down all the time, forbidding him to do anything of the sort. Things, of course, relaxed as we got to know him better and better. Half the battle of a band is trusting each other, and that started to develop."

BORDIN: "I was listening to The Last Poets (radical '60's black rappers) and Roddy was just getting into early Run DMC and alike, Johnson Crew, and he brought that into the music which was a good thing. Once again, all these different influences were there and it was great. You could play keyboards and bass in percussive ways and it was still melodic. We started doing that and seeing how it all fitted together, which was another big part of our coming together."

BOTTUM: "We had been through a lot of guitar players and singers which was kinda fun, and at the time it was the way we wanted the band. We had this oath that every show we did would be different songs with a different singer and hopefully a different guitar player. It was exciting and we did it for a long time until we started feeling that bands in our position should consider putting out a record. And to do that it seemed like, yeah, we'd need a permanent guitar player. We had Mark Bowen for a while, who was really good guitar player but I don't think he was willing to put in practice time if I remember correctly. We knew that we wanted this certain sound, a big heavy crunchy power-chord-type sound. And Puffy, through his background, knew this guy Jim who had just that sound, the whole Marshall stack power chord sound that we wanted. Unfortunately it came with the attitude, but that seemed OK at the time. It was almost this weird quasi-art statement at the time. The band we were, the obnoxious, cocky idiots that we were, to have this 'rocker' onstage with us almost seemed like a statement at the time and one that worked. It wasn't that we thought Jim was a moron or anything, he was just so utterly different than anything I'd ever experienced before or worked with. His background was very male oriented 'monster-truck-style' 3 brothers Hayward type thing, and I grew up with three sisters in this 'Hollywood' upbringing. Completely different, and then it comes down to guitar versus keyboards. It never bothered me, it still doesn't bother me to this day it's just who we are. We each cover the different ends of the spectrum as far as our band goes."

Gould counters: "The clash of opposites between Roddy and Jim is highly exaggerated, I think they have more in common than not. Their opposites are very superficial."

JIM MARTIN

Neither an apologist or a diplomat, Jim Martin has always seen things differently to the rest of Faith No More on pretty much every count. Born at Perelta Hospital, Oakland California, Martin was different from day one. A kindergarten teacher assigned Martin's class to draw a picture of their family. Martin's picture showed all of his with horns.

" My earliest memory is that of my Aunt changing my diaper whilst singing 'Strangers In The Night' to me, the part where it goes 'scooby-dooby-doo-dee-dooby'. I can't clearly remember the first music I heard it's a muddled affair, it was AM radio The Beatles, then I think of Christmas carols and whatever. But apparently before I was walking, you tend to hang around with your mother at that age, and she'd visit my Grandmother where they'd speak Spanish. So I spoke Spanish from an early age myself.

"I was very sneaky, a quiet child, and I could pretty much get away with anything I wanted to do because I was very quiet about it. So, of course, I did all kinds of evil little investigations that children do. I wasn't a subdued child but I just did things that needed to be done. I remember my Mom making me take piano lessons before kindergarten, then in 4th grade I took up the trumpet. I picked up the guitar in 7th grade, and before I knew it I was put into a parochial Catholic High School. This was actually quite a treat as only the girls had to wear uniforms, y'know a skirt and shirt. And the girls insisted on wearing them as short as possible. A wonderful but trying time in my life, because I spent most of my High School days with an erection.

"7th grade was when alcohol, music and women first came into my life, although alcohol wasn't a big deal because we'd always have a little shot of wine with dinner. But we built this clubhouse in the back of Paddy McColl's place. None of us drove, so that was the hang-out. We used to drink booze and listen to Black Sabbath, and of course we would lure young women in there and have our filthy way with them. I was inspired by the old Sabbath 8-track tapes to play guitar. So, in 1975 I got a Japanese Epiphone guitar and Yamaha 50 watt amplifier for Christmas. I was fooling around playing Sabbath and Skynyrd songs, when I discovered some boys down the street wanted to form a band. So with Dan Nogales and Kevin Costa, I started a band called EZ Street. We had a bass player called Rocky Labour and I forget the first drummer. A horrible man. We were always changing drummers I remember. Then there was all that shit with Puffy and the band.

"We'd make recordings of jams like that, and to make up a set we'd just take various portions of jams and use 'em, it was a beautiful thing.."

"So we went along. Cliff joined Trauma for a short while before joining Metallica, and I kept going the best I could with this band. Eventually it dissolved, and I was working at The Bal Teeter showing Mexican films as the projectionist during High School. Then out of High School I went to work loading the docks at US Cold Storage in Oakland High Street, loading frozen food and stuff onto trucks. 4 months later I started school in San Francisco and got my degree in electronic engineering. After that I went to work for a time-clock company, doing maintenance on the things you punch into work on and also the things at parking garages. So I'd service, repair and install that crap. I hated it, but I was passing the time between playing with a few bands and getting some money. As well as the three bands I was playing with, there were also the big huge jam sessions with Cliff Burton and Dave Donato.

" I got laid off from that job, so I ended up just jamming with Cliff and Dave and drinking liquor; we never played for anyone much, we just did it for ourselves, for total fun. Then I started painting houses for money, but all of that stuff was to support my musical and drinking habits. Me, Dave and Cliff finally did a show together, in the Bay Area at a Battle Of The Bands thing, it was right around the time when Motley Crue were happening so the trend was huge hair, spandex, eyeliner, all that crap. So all the bands had that shit and there was us; three fuckin' slobs playing this rock music. They gave us 12 minutes to play a few songs and we just played the same one for 12 minutes. We threw things into a huge, vicious turmoil. We'd make recordings of jams like that, and to make up a set we'd just take various portions of jams and use 'em, it was a beautiful thing. A lot of my ideas came from, and still come from, those jam sessions. If I wanna write music these days, I'll go over and jam with Dave, record the whole thing and pick out certain riffs. I think Cliff did the same thing, he'd pick out sections he liked for his songs. There's some Metallica songs that were born from those jam sessions, such as 'For Whom The Bell Tolls' and obviously Faith No More songs such as 'Surprise! You're Dead'.

"My next job as working at R&H Liquors in Hayward, and at that time I went around to Cliff's house and there was Puffy and Bill. I'd seen Puffy around before that, he'd cut his huge Angela Davis ['60's Black civil rights figure] afro-style hairdo off and his head was hella little compared to what it used to be. He also seemed to have humbled somewhat, got a better outlook on life. Puffy said to me, 'We should get together and jam dude.' I said, 'Fuck yeah, too bad we can't get together and play a gig.' To which Puffy said, 'Maybe we can. We had a gig lined up at the Mabuhay Gardens which we had to cancel, but maybe they'll give it back to us.' So he called up, and the guy at The Mab said, 'Yeah you can do it.' So we played that Chickenfuckers gig. I remember going down to where Puffy, Roddy and Bill were in the city, something like Shotwell and 16th Street. I went in their house and it was this huge filthy thing, shit everywhere. I didn't even wanna sit down. Apparently, Roddy was living in a closet with a mouse and all his dirty laundry that he never washed, there was just shit everywhere. We practiced a little, and by the time we did that Mab gig, opening for 45 Grave, we didn't play anything we practiced. It was a GREAT thing.

"Then it came to another point where I guess Puffy suggested me to become their guitar player. So I went down to check it out. It sounded pretty good, I liked the brutal darkness of the music. It was very different to what I knew, but I liked the darkness of it and figured I could help 'em out. So I said 'OK let's do it'. At that time I'd moved onto *another* job with a company called Simplex, where I had to cut my hair to get the job and make the money of course. I had been broke, my car was broken so I cut my hair, shaved and worked. We started recording 'We Care A Lot', and halfway through recording this lady called Ruth Schwarz from Rough Trade Records heard it. She said she wanted to put it out on the label she was starting called Mordam Records. I think we recorded everything in two weekends, put it together, she released it and I immediately quit my job as we were taking off on tour."

1984

A sense of stability seemed Faith No More's for the taking, but Mosely was already demonstrating that it could never be that way.

GOULD: "Chuck was being pretty tough. Despite things happening like they were, he wouldn't move up to San Francisco from LA for reasons that make very little sense. We'd have to send him cassettes in the mail for him to learn the songs, and he'd come up for shows without ever rehearsing them with us. We were hoping he'd have learnt the songs because it was too late if he hadn't. The worst of it was that he wouldn't always fly up here, he'd take a Greyhound. We'd be playing at nine, he'd show up at five to nine without anyone having heard from him, and we'd go right on. He'd drive us crazy, but things were going well and we all felt the better things got, the easier he might become."

"I think we recorded everything i two weekends, put it together, she released it and I immediately quit my job as we were taking off on tour."

Mosely had been in a band called Haircuts That Kill who were very popular on the LA underground scene. He'd never viewed his move to Faith No More as a permanent one. This is the reason he says lay behind him not moving to the Bay Area.

"Basically the two shows after Courtney were meant to be it. I was planning a move to Holland and was dead set on it. Then came a few more shows, then came the chance to do a record, then the chance to tour, it just sort of happened. My drummer Troy from Haircuts got really mad because we were thinking of moving Haircuts to Holland. I was meant to be temporarily filling in until they found a regular singer, and that became 'I'm gonna be in this band.' "

It's the great step that every semi-serious band has to take; get a manager. Find someone prepared to carry your can, clean your mess and do your dirty work for as low a fee as possible. You expect them to get you lucrative gigs, fat record deals and mega tours with millions of dollars guarantied at the end of it all. But it rarely works that way. In this particular case, FNM were steered to managerial assistance from Will Carpmill, who's sister Olga Gerrard worked with husband Gerry Gerrard in a management company.

GOULD: "Olga put on a bunch of shows in the Bay Area. They were called 'Go Productions' and they did things like put on the first ever PIL show in the Bay Area, they were the indie King and Queen of the time. Just to get on their shows was good enough God forbid they

"That 'first tape' materialized eventually into the band's first album."

might want to manage us, that would be too cool! We'd give tapes to Will for them to check us out, and at the time I was the band manager. My hair was cut real short just so as I looked like a manager and I could walk in and book us gigs. I had a little black book; nobody knew I was in the band, I'd just sneak around and get shows. We realized that we needed a better quality demo , and there was the song we'd recorded with Faith No Man and Matt Wallace. So w went to him and said we wanted a really good quality demo on 24 tracks. He found this place Sun Studios up in Cotati CA, we hustled together $2000 and made a tape of 4 songs. It sounded pretty slick, and we figured it could get us a record deal."

That 'first tape' materialized eventually into the band's first album. Wallace still holds fond memories of the recording process.

"From what I remember, this was one of the most fabulous recordings ever done. It was the first time the band and I could get into a 24 track studio and *do* something. I had to budget, work out the time in the studio, organize the tape, get them rehearsed. It was my first real production job and it was fabulous. We got the record done basically in 3 days. The control room was about 15 steps from where we were staying, there was one room with a kitchen and eating area, off that was a small bedroom with room for two people. You had 5 Faith No More's and one Matt Wallace crammed into this thing. But it was good, we breathed, sweated and focused our energies and attentions on this one thing. It was pretty friendly tension except for Chuck. I had met him for the first time at a party with the FNM guys. He had come up to me beyond drunk and having obviously taken or smoked something, he could hardly form sentences and was drooling all over the place. I remember wondering what the hell those guys had done. So I'm thinking, 'great this is the guy they've chosen.' He made rehearsal with the band once or twice but he really hadn't coalesced what his idea with the band was. He came in, was gonna sing and we'd overdub his vocals. He starts singing and it's this completely raspy, growelly scream where you couldn't make out any words, just this primal scream from hell. It was nice for a song, but after that you wanted more. I talked to Chuck and Bill about it, Bill talked to Chuck, and when he came back the next day he opened his mouth and it sounded like Frank Sinatra! He'd gone 180 degrees the other way, and none of us had ever even imagined he had it in him. During those first demo sessions at my studio his voice was in incredible shape, it was great. He shifted back towards the gruff stuff because the band didn't want to be too much of a pop band.

"When we were in Cotati doing that first album, everything was rolling and then it came time for Chuck to sing. What happened developed into a pattern for Chuck: everytime we were doing something important he 'developed' some kind of cold or flu. I think it was a mental thing, where Chuck didn't feel confident enough to just dive into it, he would work himself up into such a frenzy that he'd actually get a cold or flu. His nose would stuff up, coughing, the whole ball of wax. That first record, Chuck had some fabulous stuff but I had to slow the tape machine down on a number of the songs so as they would be in pitch for him because of the 'mystery ailment'. Stress was probably another major factor, as well as the ultimate thing which was an extreme lack of self-confidence. Then through some touring, he stopped taking care of his voice on the road. And that was the beginning of it."

"It was scary for me having to go and record everything in tune," remembers Mosely, "that concept was still totally out of my reach. I have a split personality in the studio. There's a difference between when I'm doing shit and when I'm totally on it. Other times I get so self-conscious of what I'm doing that it makes things really scary.

I'd get colds because of stress, I still get sick if I get stressed out really badly. But recording was fun, that 'stress and scary' shit's exciting, it's more of a challenge. But then I would get sick because I didn't take care of myself. It wasn't like I *tried* to get sick though, it just happened."

From those first recording session with the band, Matt Wallace knew his work would never be easy.

"Early on it was definitely a labor of love. I had no inkling about ever supporting myself as an engineer/producer and I did love the band musically. I felt what they were doing was really unique, and even as late as 'The Real Thing' I had no idea that they'd have a huge top 10 single. I was in it because I thought, 'wow, they're innovative and the world will probably never get around to liking them but fuck 'em.' So the fact they sold a lot of record was icing on the cake. We became friends and I was into their work. Which is why it was very gratifying that we got our first gold and platinum records together, because we'd all been through the learning process as a team."

Finding a label to release their aural madness was an uphill battle. Then came a small, unexpected but vital break from the most unlikely series of circumstances.

GOULD:"Will was working at Rough Trade back then and we gave him a tape to play in the store for people who were buying LPs. The day he did that, Ruth Schwarz [who owned a distribution business] walked in and wanted to start a label. She asked what the music was. Will told her that it was Faith No More and they wanted a deal. So she was onto me that day, saying she wanted to release our record.

"Gerry and Olga were onto it at pretty much the same time: 'Hey we wanna manage you guys.' Then three weeks after 'We Care A Lot' came out in early 1985, Slash hit us up after the person who booked the I-beam—Kathy Cohen— tipped them off. So it was suddenly

"I was in it because I thought, 'wow, they're innovative..."

boom boom boom! Kathy knew the A&R girl at Slash—Anna Stadtman—who ironical-ly enough knew Roddy from LA. She had been invited by him to a show a year earlier when she'd yelled and hung up on him; she was very rude. The first thing she therefore did was to start kissing up and apologizing!

"So, anyway, she finally came and Slash hit us up pretty hard. So we were happy, but didn't know how to draw up a contract. Our deal with Ruth and Mordam had been very above-board, straight-forward. She pretty much made enough to cover her side of things and gave us the rest. Then Slash give us this 30-page record contract, and we didn't know what the fuck to do. Timing was how it all worked out. Gerry and Olga could work out our contracts and book our tour, which they did. We had a tour in early 1985. Gerry and Olga showed up at our house the day we had to leave with this 4-door pick-up truck—a 1966 Dodge with a flat thing. We went and got a Jartrans trailer for equipment and a camper shell for the pick-up part so as people could sleep in it. Three days after we got that trailer the company went out of business, so we drove around in a stolen trailer that we never had to pay for."

The tour was memorable if only for the series of struggles that took place.
 "We had a roadie called Jim Olsen who never drove, didn't like to lift a finger for work yet demanded his $10 per diem daily. Economically and materially it was the hardest tour, because we didn't have any money, didn't have much to tour with, were humping our gear around all over night after night. But it was the most fun tour because everything was new, for years we'd wanted to tour so it wasn't so bad. The problem was that the 'We Care A Lot' LP wasn't in most of the stores when we got to these towns. We played in Jackson, Mississippi one time, and even though no-one had the record they came to see us play because nothing else much happens in Jackson, Mississippi anyway. So we had a good time there, and we ended up staying at some kid's house. Our next show was in Athens GA, about 12 hours away, and this kid had a friend there so he told us to give his friend a call and we could crash there too.

"We were so desperate. There was this pizza place where the girl who was working had pink hair, so we figured maybe she'd be cool enough to put us up.."

"So we left at 8 am that morning and drove about six hours until we were in Birmingham, Alabama. Seeing as I was the 'manager', I called the show from a gas station to make sure everything was OK. The guy goes, 'Yeah well finals start today at the University Of Athens and I haven't had time to put up any fliers for the show...maybe you don't wanna come.' We were already half-way there so we just thought 'fuck-it', drove on and loaded in around 7 pm. So I figured I'd call the guy we were going to stay with. I put him on the list, Ron Hargrave plus two, and they were the only guys who showed up! One of them bought a beer from the bar. We were taking 60% of what the bar made, which meant we made roughly one dollar! From there we had to get to Atlanta, where we had 10 days until the next show. 10 days with no money and nowhere to stay! I was calling everyone in San Francisco who had the remotest thing to do with Atlanta. There was a record cold spell that night, 17 degrees, I could barely dial the numbers on the phone my hands were that cold. We all went and hung out in a laundromat for a while, because the dryers were on and we could stay warm.

"We were so desperate. There was this pizza place where the girl who was working had pink hair, so we figured maybe she'd be cool enough to put us up. We just walked in and asked her if she would which, of course, she didn't. We didn't have our record in the store, no-one knew who the hell we were, but we opted to go to the club we were gonna play in 10 days and tell the owner Paul our story. So he let us crash on the stage at The Metroplex for a week.

" We got our PD down to $2 a day because that's all we could afford. Jim (Martin) and I weren't eating, we'd just buy 40 oz malt liquors and drink to kill the pain. So we still have no money, and we're booked to play with Ministry in New Jersey, which was quite a coup for us even though it was when they were a dance band. Steve Blush booked the show at Trent City Gardens, and we started playing. They gave us about two ft of stage space to play on, and we weren't being too confrontational, but Ministry took us like assholes immediately. They didn't like us from the start, I guess because we were scruffy, dirty-looking and they

were in standards and clean-cut. So they had this Fairlight organ or something onstage, and some guy to guard it whilst they went out to dinner. It was some ridiculous high-tech thing.

"So we're playing, thinking everything's OK, and through our monitors this guy goes, 'OK you're gonna fuck with us we're gonna fuck with you. We're gonna fuck you up, you trash our shit.' Everybody in the audience is wondering what the hell is going on, to us it's like this 'voice from God'. We can't work out what it is and we can't work out what we've done. I guess because we're a really active band, they thought we were stepping all over their stuff when we were just trying to play. I guess Chuck threw a bottle into the audience, which I didn't see, and then he started doing a strip-tease. And we started playing harder and harder; next thing I know the power's gone, guys are up onstage throwing us off-stage and getting our gear and throwing it in the alley. They threw us out without paying us the $125 we were meant to get, total bullshit! It was a case of this band picking on us thinking they'd never see us again, like, 'Who are these assholes? Get them out of here don't pay 'em.' Of course Steve Blush later gave us the money out of his pocket when we were in New York. It was people like him booking us all over, and the Volcano Sisters that

"then he started doing a strip-tease. And we started playing harder and harder.."

helped pull us through. We were meant to stay with those girls for a couple of nights, and we all ended up there for nearly a month! The day after that Ministry show we made it into New York City with, after paying tolls, a total of $2.64 cents among all of us. We got a roasted pepper sandwich and split it. That night we did a show for $750, so we were back on cash flow again. That gives you an idea of the early touring. But really what was killing us was that our album wasn't in any of the stores. That was the main reason we left Mordam to sign up with Slash Records.

"Bob Biggs (president) said that he saw what we were trying to do. He felt he could hit up some big corporate company to also see it and finance it, which for a label was extremely perceptive. I mean this is the label that started with The Germs, started Slash Magazine, so it was a very cool thing. To me it was better than being on a label like Swan Song Records, which actually may have embarrassed me. So we were happy to sign up with Slash and we had a budget of $30,000 for the 'Introduce Yourself' album."

BOTTUM: "The thing that most impressed us about him was that he had this history thing with The Germs records. He was there with the first young punk band out of LA. To be there with a guy like that, who'd taken a chance with a band like that, and who said he saw us as being similar to the Germs, was very flattering. His label pretty much symbolized what we were about, just doing the thing we did and suddenly being almost embraced by the public."

AUTHOR'S INTERLUDE # 1

I remember the first time I saw Faith No More. It was August 1986, before the band went in to record the 'Introduce Yourself' LP. I was fresh in town, having spent a month travelling from Britain to New York to SF, and Metallica's Cliff Burton was making sure I met people, made friends and got out. He took me along to The Stone, a famous San Francisco rock'n'roll club on Broadway, where his pal Jim Martin was playing a gig. Faith No More were a blur, a twisted out aural trip, something I wasn't immediately ready to take in. Special? Of course. Captivating? Without a doubt. Martin looked like a weirdo, red glasses, shortish fuzzy hair, this freak on the drums like Animal from the Muppets, and that singer. Immediately I could sense that the singer was volatile, a hit-or-miss. I told Burton he seemed like a 'liability'. We both agreed. Afterwards Burton, Martin and I went and ate some Mexican food two doors down the street. I wouldn't touch the Chile Verde; it was green food and I wasn't into that. Martin yelled repeatedly 'EAT THE GREEN EAT THE GREEN EAT THE GREEN!' and intimidated as I was, I wouldn't do it, I wouldn't buckle under to the booming voice of the weirdo in those glasses. i remember him driving a beaten up Ford Pinto, cars that were famous for their potentially lethal gas tank positioning; it was in the back of the car. One rear-end whack and your ride could go up in flames. Jim Martin would purposely drive his over rough terrain wasteland, laughing maniacally. He once mad a girlfriend of mine cry doing this.

Later on, in November sometime, I went to Bordin's apartment. he mostly huddled into his cluttered bedroom, littered with albums, clothes and some African artifacts. A huge pile of bedding and pillows sat atop his and girlfriend Marilee's bed; it looked like a perfect place to hibernate for days on end. His dreads were growing, thick puffy lumps, 'clubs of doom' as they became known, for if Bordin swung his head at you and they hit, you'd bruise. He prepared a meal, this enormous bowl of spaghetti and a big piece of steak, and we sat around stuffing our faces. Food and sleep are two of Bordin's major pleasures. He was halfway to nirvana.

1986

As the Slash deal was coming together, Faith No More discovered that their feelings towards the Gerrards were rapidly changing. They started looking more closely at what was being done for them. Conspiracy theories were abundant and soon it was summarized that the Gerrards were scheming to rip the band off. An uncomfortable and bitter situation ensued, spurred on by the naivety of both parties in their dealings with each other.
GOULD: "It was awkward because I was a homeless guy, living out of my back-pack at people's houses, and I ended up living on the Gerrard's couch. I used to stay at Roddy's house as well because he had a job and I'd crash on the floor. He worked at movie theatres selling popcorn. I was actually a janitor at one of them, the Ceaser Cinema. It was funny because there was this little punk rock scene in the local cinemas where everyone knew everyone else and things were pretty cool."

MARTIN: "They wanted to manage us so they let on the impression that they knew what was happening. They were sorta trying to appear more knowledgeable and experienced than they were, which didn't seem to sit to well with us. But I guess they did a pretty decent job. Things just got ugly after a while, pretty much escalating when Bill moved in with them. It's really not good to know business associates in such a close and familiar fashion."

GOULD: "To be honest the Gerrards were really cool. No, I don't think they were as experienced as they lead us to believe. I found out, after they'd negotiated that first contract with Slash, that it had been their first. We trusted them totally. We'd ask them questions and get put down immediately , which ultimately lead to us getting suspicious. Now I have to say I don't think Gerry and Olga ever stole anything from us, I think they were honest. I think we

were just suspicious enough, and they were naive enough to be defensive and a situation got created, an ugly one. I don't think we really knew what we needed a manager to do and they were still learning what a manager did and didn't do. So it was two inexperienced people trying to work their stuff out.

"We asked Cliff (Burton) at one time about them because they wanted 50% of our publishing. He told us that anyone who asked for any of our publishing was a thief and should take their business elsewhere! He told us we should never give anything of our publishing away And in the ideal world that's true but I later found out people end up giving 15% of it away to their management or whatever, it's a source of income. But we took that stance at the time, told them we wanted to revise the contract, and they started screaming at us about 'changing the contract' and we told them it was pretty cold them trying to take away our publishing.

"I was living with them at the time hoping that we could separate business from social life, and of course that didn't work out. We ended up firing them and paying them off for work they said they'd done, we made what to us at the time was an outrageously high settlement. And we learnt a lot, they had a ghetto blaster stolen from one of our shows and they charged us for that. Of course they might have felt totally justified, but we had no money and it just seemed they were trying to bleed us. We asked Gerry why this was happening? He said they weren't gonna go away, and sued us for $1.6 million dollars which was absolutely ridiculous. In the meantime we had Warren Entner interested in managing us, but he wouldn't touch us until that

"we all had to take loans from our parents *and* we covered Chuck's ass.."

shit was sorted out. So, we all had to take loans from our parents *and* we covered Chuck's ass. The four of us borrowed money from our parents, and I believe that he couldn't get any money. But instead of maybe pulling that little bit harder and working that little bit extra, he just carried on being lazy old Chuck. We did this before 'Introduce Yourself' came out, and we only managed to pay back our parents when 'The Real Thing' went gold in 1990, about 4 years later. We ended up being more than a little bitter about it, because we'd never dealt with the legal system before. It was basically a divorce. I get on with Gerry Gerrard pretty well these days, but Olga takes things fairly personally and I don't think she'll ever forgive us."

Warren Entner, a Los Angeles-based manager, had already experienced rock'n'roll on both sides of the fence. He had been in successful '60's band The Grass Roots, who had enjoyed a string of top 30 US hits and sold a few million albums in the process. Entner immediately saw the band's potential, and was happy to take on the band once the Gerrard situation had been sorted out. Entner was no stranger to managerial success either, having masterminded the enormous breakthrough in 1984 of Quiet Riot, an average Heavy Metal band who ended up selling 5 million copies of their debut album 'Metal Health'. His right-hand man and partner, John Vassilou, had done many tours of duty with southern rockers Blackfoot, road managing Ricky Medlocke and company in their own glory days. WEM had, to this point, been seen as a Heavy Metal management group (they also handled Faster Pussycat) and many wondered how such a union could work. Of course, for the alternative Faith No More there was immediate suspicion. However Entner had built up an impressive repertoire of contacts in the LA music industry, and in 2 years time the 'gamble' was to pay-off handsomely. When the silver-tongued approach or hefty boots were needed most, when 'The Real Thing' album would've died in less-experienced hands, Warren Entner was there to kick things along and pull things through.

Slash were feeling a little dubious about what Matt Wallace would do to the band. They didn't trust him and they didn't know the band. They thought that, perhaps, the two might waste the money and produce a piece-of-shit album unsuitable for release. So at their insistence, Faith No More also brought in Los Lobos member Steve Berlin to make sure things didn't get out of hand. Los Lobos were just coming off the back of their massive Ritchie Valens cover hit 'La Bamba' at the time. No doubt Slash were also hoping Berlin's name might help give the album an extra commercial boost.
GOULD: "He didn't do that much, but he'd just been involved with that year's huge hit which explained half the reason he was there. And he really didn't end up getting paid a huge amount of money, something like $5000. But to us that was an exorbitant amount, and we resented it."

Wallace remembers those same feelings, but looks back on the situation philosophically.
"I had no track record. I was just this indie Bay Area guy who was doing great work with FNM, but Slash wanted someone with a track record of sorts. So they got Steve in from Los Lobos. We'd rag on him, 'man Steve Berlin is just a baby-sitter', but the truth of the matter is that Faith No More and I knew what we wanted. We had focused ideas and goals; anyone else was just not in the picture. Our budget was $50,000, peanuts in the music industry, but Slash weren't going to trust it with a bunch of young upstarts. I think Slash felt if I was in charge of the money I wouldn't be able to handle it, that I'd let the band would spend it on blow [cocaine] and women. So he was brought in to keep an eye on us. What I do want to note is that Steve Berlin was incredibly gracious, something none of us realized at the time. It was obvious that I was not only engineering but also producing [Wallace was hired as engineer with Berlin the accredited producer]. He saw that we had something going between us, and he rang Slash up and told them he wanted us to be co-producers, splitting responsibilities and money. A lot of people who'd have left the situation where they were getting the money and I did the work, but he was very cool. In the end, he'd just sit back and read the papers because we'd never take his suggestions.

"The recording took about 2 weeks in Studio D in Sausalito, and we had 10 days at this cesspool studio called The Control Centre in LA; what a little dump! Then we mixed back at Studio D on a non-automated board, so I had to mark and memorize fades, etc for every song. Back then I was sharp, concentrated, and now everything's automated I don't have to be quite as much in that mind-set. Chuck was still developing these cough and everything at the time. So I pushed him through it by getting him cough syrup, telling him to get to bed on time, and not letting him smoke cigarettes or pot because he was singing. I actually got him jogging at one point to build up his lung power! *Anything* just to get him in to deliver the goods and get locked in."

1987

'Introduce Yourself' was a tremendous piece of work, unpredictable, explosive and unclassifiable. There can be no denying Mosely the eerie, haunting and melancholic spectre he managed to throw over the album with his lyrics.

41

"I think all the emotions and themes came from the emotions of the music. 'Death march' *sounded* evil to me, which is where the evil lyrics came from, but I can't really read into my lyrics too well because I just piece them together. I mostly write shit that suits the phrasing I wanna use."

America, stuck in pop-metal land, wasn't quite ready for Faith No More. The 'We Care A Lot' video got some airplay on late-night MTV, but nobody there went-to-bat for the band just yet. Europe was to prove the band and album's salvation, and any hope the band had of igniting the States was to take a huge blow at an LA 'record release' gig.

"It was when we played the 'Introduce Yourself' album release party at Club Lingerie in LA," remembers Gould painfully, "all the press and writers came down, and Chuck got drunk and fell asleep while we were playing. We didn't get written about in the States for nearly two years after that. That show set us back a couple of years in the States, and was probably another reason we happened in Europe before here. When we signed to Slash there was quite a buzz on us, believe it or not, but people were disgusted by that show. I remember getting a ride back with his cousin and saying to Chuck, 'You pathetic drunk. If you ever do that again you piece of shit, find another band, I can't believe...' just giving him the whole thing. And his cousin said to me, 'You ever talk to him like that again you're gonna have to deal with me.'

"all the press and writers came down, and Chuck got drunk and fell asleep while we were playing.."

"But that was life with Chuck. He always seemed to think, 'Hey why are you coming down on me? Be cool be mellow and everything will be fine.' But the problem was that when we were like that things weren't mellow. It's just really hard to describe how difficult it was working with this guy. I remember it because I lived it, but putting it into words is really tough.

BOTTUM: "We went down there, and Chuck just kinda passed out and fell asleep onstage. Yeah it was horrible, really aggravating. It was this sense of things being completely out of control, you couldn't have screamed at him, you couldn't have said anything that would've changed anything. It just fucked things up."

Still the band set off on a gruelling US tour with The Red Hot Chili Peppers.

MARTIN: "We did the pick-up truck tour, then we did another tour in the loading van, that Ryder Truck [the Chili Peppers jaunt]. We lived in it, no windows, the height of Summer, this little vent to the cabin, all in the American South. Basically, three months of sweating."

GOULD: "When we went out with The Red Hot Chili Peppers it was like an endurance test, 54 shows in 57 days or something like that. We fought a lot of course. But I remember particularly despising Jim around that time, to the point of actual physical blows. It all makes me seem pretty abusive but it only happened when things got really bad. It's not usually how I behave. He [Jim] was such a pig-headed sonofabitch and we were in this truck together. But that's personality, not music. Personalities were clashing for sure. Imagine Puffy, who's the kind of guy that likes to hibernate in his bunk. We obviously didn't have bunks in the Ryder truck, so imagine how he tried to escape. Blankets over him, headphones, those little eye-shades like you get on planes, totally trying to withdraw from the human race.

"It was a little easier with Chuck on The Chili Pepper's tour because I think he admired them. So he didn't wanna come off looking like an idiot in front of them. It also wasn't our show, we weren't the headliners so if we didn't deliver then no-one would've really cared. Therefore he did a good job. He's that kind of guy, when it matters he sucks, when it doesn't he's great. But we always had problems with him showing up late, being difficult, wanting his per-diem advanced 6 days ahead, asking people on the freeway where he could get pot, just stupid shit. At this point I hated the guy and I can't really give any one reason, I just hated him. But it was in Europe that things really 'took off'."

AUTHOR'S INTERLUDE #2

IT WAS 1987, a hot, sticky Summer. It was stupidly hot and humid in Hoboken, New Jersey, something like 95 degrees. Faith No More had been travelling the country in a Ryder truck, moderately sized and intended for cargo transportation only. A makeshift 'cage' had been set up in the van's left-hand corner for the equipment. The rest of the truck floor was a litter of blankets and sleeping bags, pillows and grotty clothes. No windows. No air conditioning, hell, there was hardly ever any AIR. A small window through to the driver's cabin was the only thing that offered relief. People begged to drive just so as they could hang their arm out a window and breathe. They were in town to play a joint called Maxwell's. Everyone was scattered around. Chuck was hangin' with a few of his East Coast pals, whilst Jim Martin clutched a beaten briefcase with the iron grip. It was Jim's turn to be 'tour accountant', and he was responsible for dispensing the per diem's allowable for each day's expenses. Jim and I were about to make the long walk down a hot and sticky High Street to get beer, when Chuck approached. He said something to the effect of, 'I want my PD's now.' Jim coolly replied that Chuck had received three day's worth already and couldn't have anymore. 'Fuck you,' came the reply, and Chuck said he wouldn't give up any of the band's guest passes that he had assumed responsibility for. Martin stood his ground in the face of cheap insults. I remember wondering how anyone could be such an enormous asshole as Chuck, it astounded me how selfish he was being. Everyone else seemed to be united in the general working cause of Faith No More, and here was Chuck lumbering around like a huge asshole, drunk and disorderly, spouting off at his own people. The show was spastic, Chuck all over the place, the band seemingly tottering on the edge of total collapse before pulling it together for a couple of songs.

They were back soon after, playing with the Chili Peppers at The Ritz in New York City. Roadie Ghandi had some big scissors and was threatening to cut off his dreadlocks. Roddy Bottum said he'd do it if Ghandi did it. They both chopped their dreadlocks off in the cubicle dressing room above the Ritz stage. Chuck painted his face green (it was Halloween) and put in a fantastic performance, as Faith No More tuned in and turned on. Later on that night, back at Slash record's promotion chief Michelle Zachella's hotel room, Martin and I got drunk. We ordered dinner and took off afterwards for our friend Steve Blush's apartment in the Lower East Side. It was a tiny studio, screaming with humid heat and no air conditioning, crammed with books and records. The Chili Pepper's Anthony Keidis was there with Flea, and two women, one of whom was Anthony's actress girlfriend. Gould was also hanging out. Bordin was sitting in a chair right below a towering, over-filled bookshelf. Martin and I took up position in two chairs at the end of the room and started drinking and bellowing loudly. Everyone but us had dropped some acid, and Flea spent the rest of the night with his knees hunched under his chin, staring madly at Jim and I, unable to divert. God knows what we must've looked like to him. I remember him saying something along the lines of 'the world is pouring out of my asshole.' Bordin spent four hours asking if anyone wanted to join him for breakfast before having a 'seizure' fit and flipping out, books tumbling onto his head, records falling everywhere. Finally, at 7 am, Martin and I said we'd go and have some breakfast with the Puff. We got downstairs and suggested going to a diner around the corner. Bordin wanted to walk 15 blocks the other way. We said no, why not just hop around the corner and Bordin shouted, 'OK fuck you guys I'm going THIS WAY,'

turning on his heels and storming off. Martin and I pissed ourselves laughing it was so hopelessly stupi

The British press lept all over Faith No More, relishing the chance to cultivate a brand new bunch of Cal-weirdos who ended up doing the job themselves better than most could've expected. Irony being what it is, the very first story on the band appeared in the Metal magazine KERRANG!

"We were all babbling drunks, fighting with Chuck. It was the first real interview we'd all done and we were hating ourselves.."

GOULD: "It was hilarious to be in metal mags in the same way it was hilarious for Jim to be in the band. It was almost a joke but it all worked. I remember that Jim wanted to do these guitar solos all the time and it fuckin' sucked, this suburban caveman! And this guy called Dave Katz, who Puffy later falsely started a rumour had been dead for three years, asked why the hell we had him in the band, that neither of us really saw what the other was doing. I told him that we needed a heavy guitar, and we couldn't use some alternative guy who'd been fed on U2 to supply that punch. So really it was all about cooking a brew; he fulfilled that ingredient. We didn't have to like him, we didn't have to get on or hang out with him, he was an important ingredient."

The Kerrang! piece was quickly followed by a front cover story in British music bible Sounds, and a spread in the Melody Maker when the band went to the UK for that first tour. Matt Smith's infamous interview was to prove a definition of Faith No More for longer than they expected.

GOULD: "We were all babbling drunks, fighting with Chuck. It was the first real interview we'd all done and we were hating ourselves. Then it came out and we ended up looking kinda good, so that just made things more difficult. I can't say more than it was just 'difficult'. We felt after that story that it was OK to do our laundry in public, and it was probably the worst conclusion we could've come to. Rather than thinking we got off lucky, we figured we could say whatever the hell we wanted because we were being 'honest'. That became a really bad habit. We got into slagging people at will without thinking of the consequences, and doing things because it was expected of you. But overall the vibe was really 'up' and optimistic, even if things were difficult."

1988

Around the time of the great British buzz, Mosely's already questionable attitude took a vicious turn for the worse. More drunk and belligerent than ever before, it was the beginning of the end for him.

BORDIN: "Watching Chuck at that point was nothing but frustrating. He'd show flashes of genius, sharp wit, humour, energy he was so insane. He lived in LA, he saw those shows at the Starwood and wherever. He totally had it but somewhere along the line, and for whatever reasons, he let himself down badly."

On his return from that first UK tour, Mosely was upset at some of the reviews which questioned the technical strength of his voice. Indeed, many reviewers called it as it was: Chuck Mosely was a superb frontman, unpredictable and razor-edged, but you didn't love him for his throat. Mosely swore he'd get singing lessons and start to watch himself a bit more.

Encouraged, the rest of the band gave him money for singing lessons. A couple of months passed and Chuck Mosely was no nearer to actually getting the lessons than he had been before. Mosely was seemed hellbent on wasting his talent - and getting thoroughly wasted. Finally, in early 1988, something snapped.

"He gave us hell every day since the day he joined the band," remembers Gould, "I never thought of getting rid of Chuck until one day I snapped. We'd denied it for so long and then one day in practice I just snapped: threw my bass, threw my amp and just attacked him. It was one of those things that, once you've done it, there's no going back. So I said, 'fuck you I quit'. And I quit the band right then, because I thought it was just me that couldn't handle it. Then Puffy came out with me and started talking as we drove around. I found out it wasn't only me. He said he didn't like playing with him either, it bugged the shit outta him. And I liked playing with everyone else except Chuck, so that was the first time we conceived the fact he had to go. We had the second tour of Europe coming up to capitalize on this bunch of great press we were getting. So I had to kinda eat my words and re-join just to keep Chuck in the band, and just to do the tour. But we knew we were gonna fire him afterwards.

"I mean he was acting like a dead-man! Doing quaaludes, he spent 300 pounds talking to his girlfriend trying to sort out a personal thing high on quaaludes. He attacked Jim, when Jim had a broken hand in a sling from punching out the roadie Joey. There were a few shows where I'd come off stage and immediately punch him in the stomach when no-one was looking, I remember doing it onstage at the Cat Club in NYC when the lights went off, I just punched him immediately! Before we were in the band together he was one of my best friends. Which goes to show maybe there are some people you just shouldn't be in bands with, because you look at them in a way you probably never should have. Because when someone's your friend, and you see that bad a side of them when you're relying on them, they can never be your friend again.

"There was no pain involved for any of us in kicking Chuck out, except for Roddy, which is something I still don't totally understand to this day. The thing about this band, is that we do our best not to fight and end up avoiding issues. It has to get really ugly for anything to happen, and unfortunately I always find myself being the guy who throws the tantrum when it gets ugly. Hence snapping at Chuck in rehearsal. But that was the first point of real communication we'd probably had on the whole issue. I was amazed when Puffy knew why I did it, and Jim wasn't around when it happened but he was pretty much in agreement. But Roddy had a really difficult time dealing with the fact that I could lose my temper at Chuck. That pissed me off even more, and then he didn't want Chuck to go without a band vote. He ended up taking our side, telling us we were making a really big mistake, but he did what was necessary. Roddy did not want Chuck out of the band because he's very into maintaining the status quo, regardless of how healthy or unhealthy it is."

These days, Roddy Bottum looks back on the early tour squabbles with more endearment than one would reasonably expect.
"We would always have really good fights, and I tend to look back at them fondly. People were getting drunk and there'd be fist-fights and people deciding when we were leaving and who was driving. Reaching the point of actually throwing punches was really exciting. I think the only time I ever got involved was hitting Jim once when we were in a wrestling thing, but besides that I never really threw punches. Chuck and Billy were always at each other. He punched him once onstage at The Cat Club in New York when the lights were out! Of course, the fondness is all in retrospect. At the time it was pretty difficult to go through, the fighting, the tempers, the personalities that were flaring all the time. It was all very tough.

"The ugliest scenario was that whole thing in London when Jim and Joe(Ghandi-roadie) got

into it. Joe was a really good friend of ours and no-one really knew who's side to choose. On the one hand Jim was saying Joe just flipped out, and we knew him fairly well yet had never seen that side to him. And it turned out that he did have that side to him and that's why they kinda got into the fight. An ugly scenario, and it was a pivotal point as far as letting control go to someone else. Because that was when the management stepped in and said, 'Look, y'know you guys can't use this person [Ghandi],' because the scenario was bad. If he and Jim had been fighting that whole tour, it would've been ugly. So we had to get a different roadie. We let management find the roadie, which was a very pivotal point of handing over control."

For all the aggravation, it always seemed as though Bottum was the one who went through the whole affair the most easily. Whereas Mosely managed to grate on just about everybody's nerves and evoke some horrifically abrasive results, Bottum always remained on an externally even keel.
'Pretty much. I don't think I worried about it a whole lot. I think I knew things were gonna have to change for everyone in the band to stay happy. I was the one who made the phone call to tell him it was over. I think he knew it was coming, and it was very tough because he was a good friend of mine. It only got weird later, when he had to involve lawyers and start this whole legal thing between him and the rest of us. That's the only time it got sticky and ugly. It was a stab in the back for us, kinda fucked up. I mean, none of us had made any money at that point. He was suing us and he knew we didn't have money, that we'd put it into the band, yet he chose to take the route of suing us. Looking back on it, the situation was more pathetic than anything. I don't think he was doing it [suing] out of any vindictiveness, I think it's just that he felt it was the only thing he had, the only way his talent to this day has ever surfaced."

MARTIN: "Somewhere along the way Chuck got disgusted, and he showed it in his performance. It wasn't just booze and laziness, it was definitely an attitude thing. He seemed to get sick of everybody and it showed. It got to the point where you wouldn't be able to tell if he was gonna have a good show or not. When we first started off I thought the guy was great, but then the good shows became few and far between. Even towards the end I knew the guy could do a good job if he wanted to, but it was a case of him not wanting to for whatever reason. I can only speculate as to the reason, and my speculation is that he grew to hate Puffy and Bill Gould in particular and got disgusted with the whole thing. When I broke my hand on Ghandi (roadie's) face during that UK tour, he got real upset because Ghandi was his friend. Ghandi was way outta line, he initiated the physical confrontation. After we'd had a few drinks with some folks from Kerrang! magazine, he suddenly seemed to develop Tourette's Syndrome or something, all this nonsense, swear words and general shit. I figured the guy was drunk so I just stood back. We were changing trains on the tube, and he suddenly attacked me right there in the station before running off. I took the train back to the Columbia Hotel, where I waited for him. By that time I'd been pushed beyond the point of passive restraint. We got into another fight, I broke my hand, ("Jim put his [Ghandi's] head through a wall at the hotel, there was a hole in the wall!" remembers Gould enthusiastically). He got sent home, and this was on the first date of the tour. So I had to tape my fingers together and play the tour with a broken hand."

49

That all-important British tour was sold-out. But, if there had been any lingering doubts about firing Mosely, they were to disappear quickly during the journey.

GOULD: "After Jim's fight with Ghandi, Roddy and Chuck started laying into Jim all the time until finally I threw another temper tantrum and told them all to shut the fuck up! Puffy hated it, kept it to himself and got an ulcer. I got an ulcer and had to go the doctor. It was a horrible thing, a horrible feeling, the people you're working with are working against you. And this band is a democracy, there is no dictator even though I yell a lot."

MARTIN: "At some point Chuck got very disgusted, had lots of drinks on a ferry, took lots of sleeping pills and stuff, and became like a dog with it's hair combed backwards. Very irritated, very vicious. He put himself in a stupid position during an interview later that day back in London [a Matt Smith story once more]. An emotional display, if you will, of bitterness where he wanted everybody to know about it. So he left himself wide-open for wisecracks and general band abuse. After that interview he decided to initiate a fight in the lobby of The Columbia, jumping on me and shouting, 'Fuck you Jim, you got rid of the only friend out here that I had.' He threw a bunch of clothshangers at me, and walked towards me. I knew what we were gonna do and tried to punch him with my good hand. As he was right there, I just tried to protect my injured hand. We wrestled on the floor and it took John Vassilou and Bill to pry us apart. After that tour Chuck did a few more shows which weren't happening, and we knew for sure that he had to go."

GOULD: "After Jim had been attacked by Chuck on the ferry, I remember running the road block because there was a ferry strike. We ran the road-block and all these truckers were chasing after us, so we drove on these gardens to get through them. We were driving to the hotel in London and there was this bottle of Jack Daniels getting passed around, which on top of the quaaludes was ugly. There was a photo shoot scheduled for two hours after we checked into our hotel, in the lobby, and in that time Chuck rang up the 300 pound phone bill. He was pissed off, babbling wildly, and suddenly he jumped on Jim and started pulling his hair. Jim was trying to hold his injured arm on the floor. At this point I was sympathizing with Jim pretty heavily. Here was this guy playing a whole tour with a broken hand, and he didn't complain once. I was really impressed by that, it was cool. And Jim said that if it went on like that anymore, he didn't wanna know. None of us did.

"We sold-out two nights at London's Town & Country, and Chuck was singing from behind a curtain. He wasn't even coming out onstage, he was just being a dick. He had no idea it was his last show. I think he felt people came to see him because he was a personality, and that he could then do whatever he wanted and get away with it. So the day after we got back from tour, we told Warren we were kicking him out. Roddy made the phone call. He was the only person who could've done it without screaming and yelling what an asshole Chuck was. I didn't just want him out of the band, I wanted blood because he made my life miserable. Our management knew that Chuck wasn't improving, that he was getting worse and that he was a liability.

"We had to pay him off of course, and it took us about a year to get him off our backs. He had a lawyer who was working for free and taking a cut of whatever was settled later, whilst we were paying our lawyers by the hour. He didn't care how long it took, so he wanted a bunch of quick dollars to go away quickly. The worst bit about it was that we'd always had a democracy, all for one and one for all with songwriting and publishing irrespective who did more of a particular song than another. But to get rid of him, we had to pay him a bunch of money *and* give him a fat percentage of the publishing or all the songs up until that point. That left us with the rest to split between ourselves. The only satisfaction I get is knowing that he spends the money as soon as he gets it."

Bottum feels that their time with Mosely made Faith No More less-than-popular in Los Angeles.
"To this day we still have problems playing down there. I don't think people in L.A. ever take us seriously. Up here it's different. People associate the band more with Billy, me and Mike, wheras in Los Angeles, Chuck would run into lots of writers and people who wrote for the LA Weekly and whoever. So the image down there was that Faith No More was this drunk guy, bumbling around and causing a ruccus. And when we play down there people tend to associate us with that, and not take us too seriously."

Chuck Mosely's memories of the split are, of course, rather different.
"When I got fired I was doing my best professionally. Onstage, writing and singing, it was the best that I ever did in the band. See, the first show I did with them I got totally drunk because I was scared shitless, totally nervous and shaking. But that's what makes me do *better* shit. But I was still too scared during those first shows to do it without drinking, this was for about the first year. Then, on the first 3 month tour we did, I was pretty much drunk every night. And after that we went up to Washington for 14 days, and on the way up was I think the first time I ever heard a tape of myself singing. I thought, 'Oh my God this is pathetic,' and I realized that I couldn't be drunk because I'd sound like that. From that point on, I would just have 'a drink'."
Mosely certainly doesn't view himself as a drunk drug-abuser always off his head.
"History will show you that if there's somebody you're trying to put down, even if it's only to keep yourself up, then you bring a couple of things in to try and make a situation seem like something it wasn't: to justify the end result that's being reached."

Mosely has the communication breakdown pegged, in his mind, much earlier than the British tours.
"It started basically on that first tour. Billy and Mike sat me in a room for a couple of hours trying to tell me their whole theory about their music. They were saying that it was the 'new shit', there was nothing else like it, that it was completely different than anything, that it would take over all the music. They'd say how it wasn't gonna be like any other rock band, it'd be unconventional, because they'd start off with the rhythm and Billy would do the opposing bass line. And that was gonna be their style, that was how it was going to be. The first time I finally realized they were thinking that way, was in that room right then. And I freaked out.

"I've never been like that. I like everything. I've always been that way, and I've never been one of those people who says you're gonna play one kind of music and have everything in your record collection. I like to play everything in my record collection, because those were the bands I had the most fun listening to. I thought they [Faith No More] were painting themselves into a corner at that time. I said, 'Look man, you can still play a fast, slow or melodic song, any kind of speed, any kind of style and it doesn't matter what it is. Because nobody can take away from you the fact that you're playing it. But if you just do this one thing which is what you think is right, you'll paint yourselves in a corner, so as when you try and do something different it'll get rejected.' I remember saying to Mike back then that he only had one drum beat, and I told them that the whole ['We Care A Lot'] album was one song cut up with little 10 second bits in-between. That's when I started rubbing it in, and realized that they wanted no part of my ideas on arrangements or song ideas. Even with their songs , if it was melodic or too fast, only a couple of them got by. 'Spirit' [from 'Introduce Yourself'] was one. They had stacks of shit that they didn't wanna play, because it was 'stupid' or too melodic.

"I was there to do a job and I was never asked to be a part of the band, in more ways than one as far as on an equal spiritual level too. I still liked Bill and we had our moments, but they were few and far between. But I never would've quit the band until I got rich enough to. When Troy was mad at me for leaving, he was cool for those first two shows I did with Faith No More. But then when he saw that I was putting all my energies into it, I said to him, 'Don't worry man. Here's what'll happen: in 5 years I'll either be rich enough to quit or I'll get fired.' I told him if I was rich and quit I'd buy us all equipment. And we'd go on from there, we'd take over 'cause we'd have the juice already. And if I got fired then I'd sue 'em and buy equipment that way and we'd take over that way. So I got fired, sued 'em and bought guitars for me and the guitar player and drums for Troy. But he hadn't changed, he'd just got worse and shit. He started leaving the drums all over town. I said 'fuck it', I needed some money and took 'em down the pawn shop, gave him the ticket and said, 'When you get $100 you can get 'em out.' He never did. He was bitter to the point of no return."

One of the most frustrating things about Mosely, was that everyone knew what he was capable of if he'd just apply himself. The potential for brilliance was startling, but he'd beat himself away from it every time.
"I improved as a performer all the time but I still never became a great singer. I'm not a concentrated learner, I just get gradually better by doing stuff. I've probably held myself back. I only say 'probably' because I've heard that from everybody, and I can't analyse why. I guess I'm just too casual about shit. I do have to say that I disagree on [band criticisms of] of a lot of the times that I played. I was still learning when I joined them, and the only time I'd sung with Haircuts it was 'raa raa raa' because we didn't have a singer. I was scared because I hadn't sung before. I'd played piano all my life, but you can see the keys and hit them right there. But I've never been able to conceptualize how to hit the right note."

Of course, as had been pointed out already, people didn't gravitate to Mosely for his voice, it was for his stage personna.
"I was trying to be able to sing in tune. I liked learning about shit, it made me want to be able to do it like Michael Jackson and shit. I was trying to be able to sing! I took one class of lessons for one semester, and then we had to leave for tour in the middle of the next semester. So they dropped me."

The fight between Martin and Ghandi was certainly the catalyst for all concerned, Mosely included.
"That Ghandi thing started it off. At the time I hadn't seen Joe act like that and I couldn't believe he would do the things Jim said he had. He was always the nicest guy, just doing this and that. And then shit happened, they sent him home and I was definitely all pissed off. The tour was bearable for me if I had a buddy along and then I didn't except for Roddy. But I told Roddy even before we left that I knew I was gonna be fired at the end of the tour. He asked me why I said that and I told him, 'Because they fuckin' *hate* me man!' I already knew that the only reason I was on this tour was

" it was for his stage personna..."

52

because Warren and John had already gotten their 25K or whatever in tour support. But I was always hoping they [the band] would change their minds."

The criticisms? The abuse? Mosely's reaction?
"It all stemmed from them being mad at me talking shit about them on that first tour. It grew out of all that. They couldn't take a joke. I'm the kind of person that'll say the shit exactly how it's on my mind. It doesn't have any bearing on how I feel about you overall, or whether or not I wanna work with you. That's just the way I feel right then and you'll have hear it! They couldn't take that, and it became a fighting match over who could make who spill the worst shit. But that stuff comes naturally for me. I *know* how to get to people. I just get straight there, no messing. Even if I'm working with them I can't help it. And I always felt that the tension did nothing but add to the music.

"I remember this one interview we did in Atlanta where the guy asked us about being a 'dreadlock' band because everybody except Billy pretty much had them. I told the guy 'Billy used to have them, but his Mom made him cut them off'. Just like that! From that point on he didn't talk to me. This interview had been at 2 pm right? So at 3 *am* he calls me up steaming, 'What the hell did you say that for today? You wanna talk about truth in journalism because that ain't true!' I knew it was from his Mom because I used to talk with her a lot, and one morning I called she told me just that. This chat with his Mom was right after I met Courtney. They were both dirty and smelly with dreadlocks. Billy walked into my work at Starving Students all dirty, grimy and dread-locky with a robe-thing on. I said to him, 'Damn! Who have you been hanging out with?' And then Courtney walks in all dirty and dread-locky ha ha ha! His Mom told me that she made him get a haircut because of all the kids (Gould's brothers), that she didn't want them getting lice! I told Bill I was doing it to spice things up a bit, that I never meant any harm talking shit. I was just trying to liven the interview up."

Mosely is bereft of bitterness when discussing his ex-bandmates. But he does feel a little cheated in the 'truth and respect' stakes.
"Let's put it this way. I never really did all of the things they say I did. I never took any drugs when I was in the band, except for 3 times, and they knew each time. It wasn't when we were playing or anything, it was when we were kickin' back after some tour. But everything they said, it's like they felt they had to say shit to justify all that stuff. I sued them for my share of the partnership. Billy and them should've known that you cannot fire an equal partner, you have to buy their part of the company.

"Yeah I feel cheated over the lack of respect I've been getting, so far as everytime I try to do something. Like when I'm talking to someone in the business. I don't appreciate having my reputation tarnished by them. I don't get that much respect, people here [in LA] don't respect me that much. After the '80's nobody wants to dump any cash to anything that ain't 100%, no gambling in the '90's. And anything with my name on it was a gamble."

Matt Wallace had always felt this 'change' would occur?
"I knew about it all along because Gould, Bordin and I would invariably end up talking about Chuck. I remember Gould saying, 'I'm outta here I quit the band.' It was after they'd played a show in Pasadena with PiL. They were onstage starting the set, no sign of Chuck, and literally seconds before the vocals were meant to start Chuck stumbles onstage, obviously having done something or another. He barely made it in time. They were tired of that crap, they wanted to be more professional. Bordin asked me what I would've done and I said I'd have to get another singer. I cannot over-emphasize how much every guy had this over-whelming desire to learn their instrument and perfect it. They'd practice over and over again,

wheras the only time Chuck sang was in the studio or on stage. Other than that he wouldn't work on his 'instrument'. I think that really got to the band, they were just tired of pulling around a bunch of dead-weight.

"I remember telling Chuck leading up to 'The Real Thing' ,and before they fired him, that he had to take singing lessons. 'You must learn to use your voice because you have a great one and good lyrics,' was what I said, but he was smoking pot and drinking all the time, really thrashing it. He took up lesson for a bit at some junior college in LA and I'd even given him the $40 for the lessons. He went the first couple of times and then came the excuses, 'couldn't get to the bus' or whatever. It didn't work out. Ultimately, Chuck's lack of confidence was so strong that he couldn't rise to a lot of occasions. If he could've conquered that, he'd probably still be in the band. It got to the point where he'd become a liability. It was safer for him to say, 'I'm a fuck up, always have been always will be.' The friction then was that the band was poised, ready, hungry and working very hard to gain the success, and Chuck was like 'I'm just not up for it I don't feel I can do it.' Meanwhile, the other guys are working 24 hours a day to get there.

"The band had ultimately decided before they asked me, and I added my opinion. I don't think my voice swayed them, but just having an outside opinion similar to theirs probably made them feel even better about it. Of course it was Bill who was the main catalyst. He's always been the catalyst for change. Bill is the clarion for the band. What the band is feeling, Bill will say it. Whether it be Mike Morris, whether it be Chuck Mosely, Bill's the guy who'll say, 'Fuck this I'm outta here,' and he's the one who forces the band to grow. It's obvious that's accurate, otherwise Bill would've been out on his butt."

END OF 1988/ START OF 1989

No-one bothered to waste too much time. The band immediately took off to regular rehearsals and jam sessions, spending nearly a year writing new material as well as planning to find a new singer.
GOULD: "We just went on ahead the four of us, sat down and wrote 20 songs right away. Everything was working great. We didn't know what we wanted singer-wise, and I'd never met or seen Mike Patton. All I knew of him was this Mr Bungle tape, and I felt advised against him because I didn't want some big fat guy that Jim could drink beer with as our singer!"

Martin had initiated the Mike Patton-Faith No More connection long before 1988 came around. The Northern Californian band Mr Bungle that Patton was a part of, had released a demo tape titled 'The Raging Wrath Of The Easter Bunny' in 1986. It was a roaringly twisted and brutal collection of the stupidest metal riffs Patton and his friends could wrench out. But Jim Martin was sold on the ridiculous tape, and would often play it late at night in his Hayward den whilst having a few beers.
"He didn't get the tape directly from my hands NO, God NO!" shouts Patton horrified by the thought, "it always kinda makes me wonder, because he likes maybe 5 or 6 bands in the whole world. So why would he like Mr Bungle ever in any form? It may well have been a savage tape, but the world is filled with savage music so why would he like this one? I always wondered about that, right to this day. How does Mr Bungle fit in with Pink Floyd,

Black Sabbath, Led Zeppelin, the DUNE soundtrack, the PLATOON soundtrack and Celtic Folk music? I don't get it, although it was obviously some weird misfortune, a twist of fate. It shouldn't have happened that way, but he was the only member of the whole band who liked that tape. He took it under his wing and started calling my house all the time.

'I didn't know who this fucking guy was [spat contemptuously]! They still had Chuck in the band, but he'd just leave messages on my parent's answering machine saying, 'Your fuckin' tape man, this fuckin' tape is the hugest, the fuckin' 'Raging Wrath...' is,' just talk like that, and I kept on wondering who this fucking goon was? I kept on thinking, 'Stop calling me.' Then he identified himself one time, and I matched his voice with the other messages."

> "Your fuckin' tape man, this fuckin' tape is the hugest.."

Patton was the first person to audition for the vacancy left by Mosely, and there was never really any doubt that the job would be his.

GOULD: "As I said I was against the idea. But then he came down and tried out. We told him to just sing with our music, whatever the first idea off the top of his head was to just sing it, and he had a million ideas. He totally understood what we were doing in a real physical sense. He took cues off the music and sang over it. We tried out a few other guys, but he was the one although I felt a bit guilty about it. Guilty because it seemed too easy. It seemed like he was gonna get exploited to death; a young innocent with long hair. Too easy to sell! But he could sing, he knew what we were doing and he was the most natural choice."

MIKE PATTON

Far from being the pretty-boy jockhead that MTV teen-mag-land 'created', Mike Patton is a complex, cynical and engaging young man with a dark-side rarely let loose. His childhood was a series of fears, all jockeying for pole-position in his life. 'Good God, my childhood was very uneventful. I remember mostly just being scared of everything. Scared of not getting good grades, scared of not going to school, just a time spent jumping from security to security. Staying at home with my parents on Friday nights rather than going out with friends, riding freight trains by myself. I have a brother, but at that time we weren't close at all. It was more like, 'I'm this way stay away from me.'

'I was basically too afraid to be nasty. I was also too afraid of doing well and being good, so that meant mediocrity was a great place for me to be. Like, I wanted to be a weatherman [laughs]. I used to pretend I was a weather man! I had all the numbers for the weather channels, for floods, off-shore reports and so on. I'd call the previous day and remember them for the next day so as I could draw up my own weather forcast. And I'd tell anybody who cared to listen what the weather would be, my parents anybody. Then cable came along and blew everything out for me, but I ended up falling in love with the weather channel!

'I didn't even want to travel. I was scared, yet I hated Eureka and Humboldt County. It was very confusing, and everything wound around to being a self-fulfilling prophecy.

of sorts. I just didn't like it there at all. There was absolutely nothing to do, yet I knew I'd be leaving at some point in my life to do something. But there was this definite lack of ambition, and even having a band was an avoidance tactic. Avoiding making friends, avoiding girlfriends all that stuff. There was a huge fear of failure and anything I did was a replacement for something else."

Patton hooked up with his friends in Mr Bungle at school, none of them being particularly deviant types at such a tender age.

"The deviancy thing came by default, getting out and seeing things, doing things, having people tell you things. Everything I did was normal to me. I mean, what the fuck did I do wrong? You do not grow up in a town like that without dents in you from living that life. An environment like that *creates* things like death metal, that sort of music doesn't come from anywhere else. Eureka has two sides: the entertaining side of pig-ignorant rednecks, there's a big timber industry up there with dozens of logging companies. But also there's a college town right near by, Arcadia. So you get all these hippies, or people who wanna 'get away from it all', who come up and go to school and study and become professional students. They come from the big cities, San Francisco, Los Angeles all these people go up there. It's like this big magnet for patchouli-scum. And both types of people live off each other, one half would shoot the other half, it was great. There was always someone to fuck with and torture.

"I remember when the Gulf War was on, Trey [Mr Bungle guitarist and pal] would walk around town with a turban on and get tons of shit. I mean, a big crisis up there was when Earth First members climbed up old trees to prevent loggers from cutting them down! Then the loggers cut the trees down, the Earth Firsters fell and went to jail for trespassing. Then the next day they made the front of the papers for police harrassement, because when they went to jail the police shaved all their dreadlocks off! Beautiful."

An environment like that was destined to breed cynical youth like Mike Patton and friends. Thus came 'Raging Wrath Of The Easter Bunny' from a small studio and into Jim Martin's hands.

"Faith No More played Eureka soon after that in a pizza parlour place we played dozens of times. There were 6 people there and 3 of them were my friends. It was really bad, a really pathetic show and I remember them standing around the van really upset. Puffy was really uptight wanting to know where to get weed. Nobody was talking to him, I think he asked us because we were just hanging around. But their situation then never even registered with me, touring was unreal, Warner Bros was like a Tom And Jerry cartoon. At that time I didn't wanna know about any of that shit. I gave them a tape and told them, 'This is what music from around here sounds like, from this region.'

"I never heard from him [Puffy] and the next time we saw them was when they played with The Chili Peppers in San Francisco. I remember it was one of our first San Francisco experiences, y'know, 'Oakies go to the big city' thing. It was a fuckin' nightmare! We were gawking around like we were on Mars. We were going to a big show in the city, we were driving, no parents, no chauffeur, and we parked right outside The Fillmore in an ugly neighbourhood.

We came outside after the gig and our tyre had been slashed. We were staying with Trey's grandparents ,who were preachers, so we changed to the spare and drove to his grandparent's place, left the car and decided to deal with it the next morning. Where we came from, you parked where you wanted, but I guess we'd parked in someone's driveway and the car was gone. So we thought, 'someone's stolen our car!' God-fuckin'-dammit, we hated the place, we hated the people, we just wanted to leave! We called the police and they told us to try City Tow, which we didn't understand. What had we done to anyone? It was, of course, there and the tyre had gone flat again. They wouldn't tow us to a service station. They just wanted us out. We found a tyre place nearby and just got the fuck outta there. I remember we were just yelling at people, yelling anything at them 'YOU SUCK!' We were driving across the bridge, all bummed out, and I looked over to my right and in this BMW was a business man jacking off! He was waving his dick at us, grinning, and it was like, 'FUCK! LOOK AT THAT FUCKING GUY!' We were his stimulus, young country boys! We got the full city treatment.

"We only came back to the city for shows. We saw Venom and Metallica once. I suppose I was just living a miserably content life, knowing there was nothing I would be able to do about it and not willing to go out of my way to change it at all. I never thought or planned anything, I never looked through any 'big windows' like that. Even now I don't, I think it's a big fuckin' mistake. I don't WANNA know!"

But it did happen anyway, despite Patton's miserable contentness. Puffy placed the phone call that steered Patton out of Humboldt County.

"Yeah Puffy, the band diplomat. And I think the reason I did it was opportunity, to have a laugh, I'm not sure. I know my first reaction was 'I can't'. I was going to school, I was in a band, maybe I could do it on my Summer vacation but I didn't want it interfering with what I was doing up there. As I remember, Puffy was greasing me in a peculiar way like,. 'We really like your tape and we're thinking of a couple of guys, maybe you could come down and practice.' I got off the phone with the guy and immediately got on the phone with Trevor [another friend and Bungle member] and told him the funny joke. 'This guy from Faith No More called me and asked me to join and of *course* I'm *not* going to do it.' It was like someone calling and saying, 'hey wanna work in the mail room at The White House? Yeah, right, what are you talking about?' I was very negative towards the idea. But I knew the band and knew there was no way I could fit into that scheme of things. I liked their second LP 'Introduce Yourself', but the first one was just bad hippy music. I hated it.

"The guy who egged me on to see them was Trey, who really liked their first record. And somewhere along the line I thought it wasn't going to hurt to do this. I felt it'd be an interesting musical experiment, it was two separate worlds. I didn't want it to be an audition thing though, 'here let me sing your songs'."

At the band's rehearsal space in Hunters Point San Francisco, the audition didn't happen like that.

"It ended up being OK. They'd play me this riff they were thinking of and just ask me to sing something with it. So I'd just start singing something that came into my head. It was hard to say whether it was good or bad, but it turned out to be a positive experience. I had, up to that point, never played with anyone else in my life. It was like having the same girlfriend for 20 years and all of a sudden seeing someone else too. So anything that was different, for better or for worse, was certainly eye-opening. But I don't think it went particularly well or anything.

"Let's face it, Mr Bungle cannot write songs. We've never been able to write songs. Everything we've ever done has been like LEGOS, wheras their stuff were real songs, verse/chorus, structured, rock music. It was so weird to me. So for me to try and sing in that way was funny and challenging at the same time. I even brought Trevor down with me because I was a little nervous. He was laughing at me singing, he'd never heard me 'sing' before because all I ever used to do was scream. Which is, funnily enough, what they hired me for. That was the only thing they'd heard. If I was to take out an ad, all that would be on it would be 'growling, shouting'.

'So for me to try and sing in that way was funny and challenging at the same time.."

"So leaving the audition I'd had fun. I didn't think much about it, because it just didn't seem possible to me. When the time came to make a decision, I said 'no' before I said yes. I told them I couldn't do it because Mr Bungle was getting interest from the only label we ever got interest from. I thought I was going to get a deal with Bungle and had no idea that smoke was being blown so far up my ass it was blurring my vision. I was impressed that a record executive flew up to Eureka on a prop-plane to see where we lived and what we were about. He was Cliff Cultreri, this great guy, a New York gangster-type from Relativity Records. He took us out for shrimp or something, was telling us how he had lunch with Zappa every Thursday and were just like, 'Wow, can't believe it, what's a guy like you doing in a place like this?' So having that in mind, why would I wanna jump into another sewer when I was happy enough in *my* sewer?

"So I thought, 'Goddamit, I'm gonna quit school and try to join this other band.' I rationalized things to myself by seeing Faith No More as school, which would still leave me with time for my other band. A stupid way to think of it. You can't think of things like that. You can't think of things like 'study' and recess' and the only way it worked out like that was because it *had* to. But I realize that having that in your mind is wrong, you cannot put things like that on scales. Of course, later on I did use it against those guys, I did use the scales. But I had to do that for myself in a weird kind of way."

Patton's initiation into the band wasn't easy. His early days in San Francisco saw him cloistered with the unique Bordin, and no-one else taking any great interest to socialize or mix with him.

GOULD: "We told Patton if he wanted the gig he had it. So he moved down from Eureka to live with Puffy. Now remember, he's never been out of Eureka and Puffy's a reclusive hermit. So Patton spends three disoriented months living at Puffy's house, he's never lived out of his parent's house, he's 5-6 years younger than Puffy and based the way people lived in San Francisco on what he saw of Puffy's way of life! He'd give Puffy rides everywhere because Puffy didn't have a car. Puffy's the kind of guy that if there's a new person to work with, he's the first one there, gets on them right away. He comes across as the contact member of the band, he's the guy who's got the objective opinion, who'll tell you anything you wanna know and is basically 'they guy'. It usually takes four or five months for the truth to come through the cracks, and after a year people usually know what's up. But those first four months are loaded with double-messages, which you keep to yourself until you talk to someone else who knows and then you understand. And Patton's a scared kid. He didn't know where to go, and none of us ever gave him a call to hang-out because he was different to us. So he was all alone with Puffy, who took him in under his wing like a father showing his son the ropes. I remember one night Patton staying at my parent's house after a gig in LA. I asked him, 'So what's it like at Puffy's house?' And he said it was OK, and I asked him if he was kinda weird. Patton said, 'No he's OK...well, now you mention it he is kinda weird.' Within 20 minutes he was yelling 'FUCK THAT GUY, WOW! THAT MOTHERFUCKER!' He didn't know how we could let him stay there for all that time with Puffy. He didn't have a chance. We had all been laughing at the thought of him staying at the Puff's house. We were probably too self-obsessed with our own thing to pay attention to his concerns and problems. It was case of, 'Can you do it or not? Are you with us or not?' Plus, we were so used to abusing each other that it never hit us properly. What a break in for the poor guy."

PATTON: "It was like living with a bag-lady. Back then he was more of a manipulator than he is now. It was interesting and it didn't take long to see the patterns. Bill would ask me if I'd seen a certain expression or been asked a certain question. I'd tell him, 'Yes he does that as a matter of fact, why, how did you know?' Then it was all clear. As people, and this is all of us not just Puffy and I, we didn't know each other very well. There was no solid ground ever, because we hadn't established any real relationship with each other either personally or musically. It was like 5 strangers in a room *always*. What the fuck are you gonna talk about? What the fuck are you gonna do, sit in the corner and cry about it or get on with things? It took how many years for things to happen. It's learning to live with someone. You fart in front of them, walk naked, you have no shame anymore. You let them see your fat parts."

'The Real Thing' was recorded once more at Studio 'D' in Sausalito California, and was once again engineered by Jim Vereecke. It was Patton's first recording with the band, one where he came in and wrote most of the lyrics.
"They had skeletons already there for some of the songs," he explains, "but others I had much more input on. I'd hear things over and over and come up with something. Lyrically nothing made immediate sense. It wasn't throwaway garbage shit, but looking back at the process involved getting there it was very careless. I thought about it like I thought about homework. That band really was school to me for a while."

Matt Wallace's first impressions of Patton as both a Faith No More member and a talent were instant. Having been, ironically enough, hired on by Slash Records

"He'd pull out all his lyrics, which were sometimes really sick. Like that song 'Underwater Love', which is really about drowning his girlfriend, and being very graphic about it.."

as their house producer, Wallace had somehow received a Mr Bungle tape himself. He too had tipped off the band that Patton may be their answer. Once the move was made and work on 'The Real Thing' began, Wallace was even more impressed.
"I think he gets big points because he came into a situation not only where the band had been together for a long time, but also where a whole album was already pretty much written. One of the most difficult times to write lyrics for music is when the album's done. So he bent and shaped his lines and lyrics to fit finished Faith No More music. With his input the band took great leaps and bounds. Within two weeks, he'd written all the lyrics to that album. With Chuck, it may still have been a very very good record because Chuck is very good lyrically. But it wouldn't have been *that* record. Patton brought clarity and diligence to the band's work. He saw their form, and he wanted to work his ideas into their format to a point where it also pleased him. There were a number of times when Patton and I met at ZIMS Restaurant in San Francisco during that LP. He'd pull out all his lyrics, which were sometimes really sick. Like that song 'Underwater Love', which is really about drowning his girlfriend, and being very graphic about it; 'his fingers down her throat' and so on. I suggested that he make things a little more obtuse, not as obvious.
The other one was, of course, the tonality of his voice which we went round and round on.

Michael Patton is one of the very few people I know who's built to sing. He has the chest, lung power and throat to go from a whisper to scream and back night after night without thrashing his voice. He also has an incredible ear for being on pitch. His voice has never blown out, and this is all physical. The guy's *physically* built to sing. He was born to do it, that's his job.

"So he has this lovely voice. I'd hear him open up on certain things and really sing. Then he'd spend a lot of time constricting it, doing that nasely crap, which really pissed me off. But the great thing was that his voice would polarize people. You either hated it or loved his adolescent whining. I'd ask him to use his voice, to please sing and he'd say, 'I can't this is my style,' which used to piss me off!"

Gould remembers the pure excitement in having a working partner for a singer.
" When we were looking for a singer, we were just looking for anybody at all. We figured if they could just hear what we were playing, if they were musical enough to sink into what we were doing then it'd be OK. The majority of singers didn't have a clue. They didn't hear what we were hearing. Patton already had ideas in his head when he came and tried out with us, and I could tell that what he was doing was on the right track. I had always hoped Chuck would sing a little more soulfully, because I felt that our songs had that potential and it wasn't being used. That was the angle that Patton took, and that's exactly what convinced me. It blew my mind how quickly he came up with lyrics for the songs. I have tapes of the early four-track stuff and it was really cool, really exciting to hear." "

The other major change between 'Introduce Yourself' and 'The Real Thing', was the guitar sound of Martin. Having moaned and complained about his recorded guitar tone to the wrong ears over the past few years, this time Martin set about doing something about it himself. Once Wallace caught wind of Martin's displeasure he was more than happy to help.
"Jim finally complained about his guitar tone, so we took off on advice of a friend of his to see Rick Rubin in LA," Wallace explains.
"We were looking for his advice. He was working with Wolfsbane at the time. I didn't get a whole bunch out of that particular trip, but it did get Jim and I talking a lot more which was great. I think [James] Hetfield helped him a lot with his tones, and I researched too. We spent two days getting the guitar tone, and we had twenty-six mikes up at one stage to find the tone. We settled on six mikes that we really liked, and the rest we left up for show. We got some of that 'POLICE LINE DO NOT CLOSE' tape and put it around the mike set-up. I felt that it was going to be another great album which would get royally ignored by everyone again."
Matt Wallace was nearly right. It was another great album, this time given the thicker edge of fat guitars and the added lust of real vocals. But it wasn't to be ignored by everyone. Far from it...

Patton's second show with the band, at the San Francisco I-Beam Club, was a video shoot for the song 'Out Of Nowhere'. A few people were distressed at Mosely's firing and came out to tell Gould and the rest just that. The few angry fans seemed intent on watching Patton come down in a blaze of shit. In the event he managed to smash his hand on a beer bottle, lacerating some tendons.

PATTON: "I just remember not knowing what I was doing, just doing anything really, the first thing I could."

Bottum remembers feeling a sense of trepidation over Patton's arrival, and what he would have to deal with being in the band.

"It was a walking on egg-shells feeling wondering how Mike Patton was gonna deal with this, because he was a really naive kid. I wasn't even that naive when I was his age. He was this kid just out of home, in his bicycle shorts and I couldn't really relate to him. And he was volatile in the way that everything affected him. We knew that things we were gonna come into contact with were gonna set him off, and we worried that he was going to be a kid who wouldn't be able to deal with the pressures as they came up. It scared me. I remember being very careful around him, realizing that anything could set this kid off and set us back a couple of years. Everything seemed on the brink of a huge temper tantrum with Mike Patton. Today he deals with things much better, but back then I think he was a lot more volatile. Especially in the early part of the tour, because we came into high focus. Suddenly we were doing the Metallica thing, and we had never done anything quite that big ever before."

Gould remembers how hard it was just communicating.

"Patton was a hard guy to talk to, really quick with his temper, but he was great. He's got a really short fuse, BAM and he's over it. But we all have slow fuses, when ours go it takes us a long time to get over stuff. We'd never dealt with that, so that was kinda weird."

With no big bands jumping to take them out as a support act, Faith No More immediately headed off on the US club circuit.

"The Real Thing' was a critical success. The usually hostile and vindictive sea of music hacks enjoyed and appreciated the album's uniqueness.."

GOULD: "The early part of touring for 'The Real Thing' was fun but tough financially. We didn't have houses to come back to, we couldn't afford the rent, so I pretty much kept my stuff at my girlfriend Christine's house. Patton had come from the security of living with his parents. He was thrown straight into this hand-to-mouth situation, where you're saving per diems and making calls from the lobby of hotels rather than pay a 25 cent usage charge. ."

MARTIN: "I was happy to a degree on 'The Real Thing' tour, but there was this general feeling of 'when is something going to happen?' We did that first part of the tour in a Ford passenger van with a trailer."

'The Real Thing' was a critical success. The usually hostile and vindictive sea of music hacks enjoyed and appreciated the album's uniqueness. An early sign of the peer respect to come was seen at the band's record release party in LA. At the Roxy, whilst the band played their set, Slash and Duff from Guns n' Roses were watching, impressed and enjoying the show. When it came time to do 'War Pigs', both jumped up onstage and jammed the song with them. Guns N'Roses were going through the roof themselves at that point, and this spontaneous appearance of Slash and Duff raced around town. Then, from out of nowhere, a break was offered to them by Metallica. A month's worth of West Coast dates supporting on their sold-out tour of outdoor amphitheatres and arenas. Many people pointed to Martin's friendship with Metallica frontman James Hetfield as the sway-factor, but Martin has no doubts as to who he feels is responsible.

"If you really wanna get down to how it happened, I believe that Cliff Burton is somewhat responsible for supporting the band when he was alive. For pushing them, pushing us all, and who knows if they'd ever have noticed us otherwise. At that time we were a virtually

unknown band in the USA, so Metallica took it upon themselves to take us on a little tour. They figured it would be fun and I thought it was. We played to a whole bunch more people and we got experience in that situation. The thing I liked about Faith No More, was that whatever the occasion, they would rise to it. Even if that meant rising up to adversity. I remember in Salt Lake City it got pretty bad. Some of the band started talking about Mormons, and of course Mormons are known as coming from that city. They all wanted to see Metallica, we came on a largely unknown band and they wanted us to get the fuck outta the way. At one point Bill decided to play a bass solo because the attitude was so shitty, and it consisted of one note over and over for something like 5 minutes. There was this amazing rain of spit coming down on Bill, we gave him the stage and he was happy to take it. We were in a position to offend because there was pretty much nothing else going for us. Nobody liked us, so it was tough shit all round. I still don't think everybody likes us."

GOULD: "The Metallica tour was cool because it was a rock experiment. No-one knew who we were, we were just thrown out in front of a lot of people. That was the pioneering spirit! It was only a month long and most people wanted to see Metallica and not us, so it was a challenge. We had to prove something. We didn't even sell any records off that tour."

Things became increasingly confusing. The Red Hot Chili Pepper's frontman, Anthony Keidis, made some sly remarks about Patton. He felt Patton was 'aping' certain aspects of his stage performance. This came down as the touring became exceptionally intense and Patton was in a whirlwind of amusement.
"Well it had to be amusing, it had to be funny. Shit like that [with Keidis], exterraneous bullshit, fringe crap. 90% of what we do is bullshit, and that bullshit is *waiting* to get in. Your duty as a musician is to be a stupid, pathetic fucking loser and take whatever people give you. Do it as easily as you can, as cheaply as you can, 'everything's paid for don't worry about a thing,' and the only way to realize that is to *be* placated and to *be* treated like that. It happened to us."

Faith No More were now everything they never wanted to be; a rock band. A funk rock band. H-E-A-V-Y M-E-T-A-L.

There were two tours relatively successful tours of Europe, before the band and it's European agent Derek Kemp wanted them back there one more time. The British record company, London, said they didn't think it was such a wise idea. The band went on regardless.
GOULD: "It was really a conversation between the management and the record company more than us. But we'd sold out clubs over there, gone back to do a slightly bigger tour which they said, 'Don't come out,' for and when *that* sold-out then they caught on. At that time, touring was at a pretty stable level. Economically it was all becoming a pain in the ass. We hadn't made any money, I didn't live anywhere when we were touring, I still lived out of my suitcase and at Christine's house. It was totally fucked in that sense. We'd save a couple of bucks here and there just to have money when we got back off tour. The band was great, but the day to day reality and what you have to live with is what affects you. You see yourself on a magazine when you're eating the cheapest McDonald's hamburger, and you tend to not give a shit."

Indeed, whilst the press were all over them, whilst Europe was falling fast for them, Faith No More still couldn't get a shot in the USA. The albums stood at approximately 30,000 copies sold in December 1989. By the time the band had agreed to release 'Epic' as their next single in January 1990, there was a sense of caution-to-the-wind. A Warner Bros head honcho, hey, maybe even Bugs Bunny himself, was a huge fan of the album. He had sworn early on to do all in his power to help break it in the States. Entner and Vassilou had a series of meetings with this mysterious supporter, and suddenly 'Epic' the video was getting heavy MTV rotation play. The rumour was that maybe 'Bugs' had placed a not-too-polite phone call, indicating displeasure at MTV's attitude to the band, and pointing out that their relationship may be soured if Faith No More didn't start getting some serious support. These speculative reports were never confirmed or denied.

WALLACE: "The one thing that band definitely did to break it was tour for one and a half years solid. The 'Epic' video had been done under the guise of MTV. They'd said, 'If we have some say in the editing we will play your video.' The band said fine, MTV loved the video yet two or three months later they'd only played it a couple more times."

In many instances the world's greatest music never reaches Iowa or Idaho precisely because those bands lack the sort of big league bullshit 'muscle' to force them into main-stream outlets. No longer would Faith No More have to worry about that. With Warner Brothers and Warren Entner applying boots and massages wherever necessary, the big wheels were turning.

1990

A short theatre tour with Voi-Vod and Soundgarden took place in the US, but Faith No More's opening slot was beginning to look increasingly out of place. Then came a Grammy Award nomination, 'Epic' getting nominated for the Best Heavy Metal/ Hard Rock' award. Between January and July1990, the video for 'Epic' was on MTV at least five times a day. By March, 'The Real Thing' had sold 500,000 copies in the US and been certified gold. This was no coincidence. MTV was packing the power to deliver Faith No More's quality punch. They went back to Europe yet again, and this time reaped the rewards of their over-whelming British success with headline shows at London's Hammersmith Odeon and Brixton Academy. The latter show was recorded for a video called 'You Fat Bastards', and a live album titled 'Live At Brixton' that nobody from the band was too keen to see released. Success was finally belting them hard in the face, and everybody was quick to tell the band all about it At every given opportunity they'd hear how 'well' they were doing, from friends to journalists to business people. Only no-one in Faith No More was having a particularly great time. What's more,
Faith No More were now everything they never wanted to be; a rock band. A funk rock band. H-E-A-V-Y M-E-T-A-L.

AUTHOR'S INTERLUDE #3

It was all so deliciously exciting. You always felt that Faith No Mores should 'break', but this being an industry of thieves, liars, cheats and assholes, you couldn't be sure. 'Epic' the video was on my MTV at all hours of the day and night, lightning-crackled visages of Bordin, Gould, Martin et al becoming household scenery. Then came the announcement that the band would travel to Britain and headline the Hammersmith Odeon. Although in the Bay Area since 1986, the Odeon had special memories for me, a place where I'd seen many bands during the late '70's/early '80's, a place synonymous with being the home of the biggest touring acts.

In the end of it all, that Odeon headliner was a disappointment. Martin's guitar was ignored in the house-sound and the venue didn't carry the magic I'd remembered it having. Seats in the stalls seemed more restrictive than ever, and large steroid cases in yellow security shirts beat the crap out of anyone breathing in the aisles. The band were to headline the next night at the Brixton Academy, a venue known but not fabled. That was to change.

The Brixton show was sheer electricity. The heaving throng of packed, sweaty fans screaming 'you fat bastards' motivated the band to hit live heights they rarely matched for the rest of that tour. And more than anything, there was a sense of 'bond', camaraderie amongst the five band members, excitement as pure as you could have. Whatever whinges and moans they were to get through in the coming months, Faith No More that night at Brixton were alive, a proud statement of how the unclassifiable could bust through. The few lowly scumbags dumb enough to write them of as 'Chili Peppers clones' shriveled in embarrassment. More than anything I remember dancing and moving and shaking amidst the sweat with my friends Mary, Ann and Neil for the whole set. I hadn't done anything like that for too long to remember. It was like watching Goliath beat the shit out of David, rip off his head and piss on the remains.

Late that year, after another UK visit and a quick sprint to Scotland to Nessie, Jim, photographer Mark Leialoha and I went back to Mary, Ann and Neil's house. There Jim Martin finally revealed 'The Puffy Files', a printed document containing over 20 detailed pages of 'Puff like activities' that had been observed during the tour. Gould, Patton and Bottum had all contributed to Martin's manuscript along with various observers. 'Puffy' had become a legendary, fabled figure. Of course it was all absurd, but so in many ways were this whole outfit. A series of arguments waiting to happen, a collection of chaos always exploding, Faith No More were senselessly unpredictable in every facet of their lives.

As with anything these bastards have ever got rolling, the whole situation threatened to get wildly out of hand. But credit to him, Puffy knew all this was going on and simply took it on the chin. I remember him telling me that, "I know what I need to do, what I need to have. A little food, some sleep, some peace and quiet, that's all, that's all." And everyone dealt with the weirdness of everything in their own way. From being a bunch of bums playing to a few disinterested people, Faith No More were the world's darlings. Fans flocked to them with weird requests and made the band increasingly uncomfortable. Well, how would you feel if a groupie came up to you and *demanded* that she lie in your bath-tub naked whilst you pissed on her? The insanity of it all may just make *you* do it as well...

"What we saw when we started getting into the rock press was an angle that had never been explored," reasons Gould, "we'd always been an alternative band, so it was a new place to go. Unfortunately, the people who were doing our stuff weren't as aggressive in other territories as they were in the hard rock one. We should've been in soul, alternative and other markets to the point where we could pull it off in all ways and styles. Unfortunately the rock one bit, and all the energies and career direction of the band went into the rock world. We didn't really feel the brunt of that until we were deep in it, and then it was too late. The only person who didn't mind was Jim, because he'd always wanted to be in a fucking rock band,

neither did Puffy probably. But the rest of us? No fucking way!

"Then it became OK to do things like Metal Forces magazine interviews because it was different. And we could appreciate people from totally different background liking what we were doing. It was even educational for me to an extent. I started to actually like Black Sabbath and even some Led Zeppelin, because if these people liked them and us there had to be some value in it. My mind was opened up a lot. But we still ended up becoming a 'category' without really knowing it. We weren't familiar with how that shit worked. We became a funk-rock band, and we knew it because on tour we'd get these funk-rock demos. It was bad, people who used to play Heavy Metal playing funk, and looking to us as their peers. It was funny!"

But the continuing news of their success wasn't. To the outside world, anybody moaning about their album going 1,000,000 platinum is being an absolute arsehole. There were many of the view that Faith No More were role-playing a 'petulant fuck-you brat-pack' image to the hilt. The truth was far more confusing, and it all revolved around the time the penny dropped for them. The realization struck them that Faith No More had sold a million albums-plus, were a huge band and were all over MTV. They had become the year's hip kids on the block.

"All the stuff happened on tour in Australia," recalls Gould, "we'd been on tour for 14 months when Warren came up to us and said the LP was top 20 in the States. He told us it was happening and that they needed us to stay on tour for another 6 months. We were really burnt out, beat, and all we saw was more of the same. Maybe we got a platinum record, but when were we gonna get a cheque for this shit? Why should we work that hard, tell me why, what would we get out of it? Maybe it looked good on paper but we didn't know who was making what out of it. That was our attitude. The photographers who were photographing us were making more money than we were. Everyone in the industry was getting rich off us, but we weren't getting rich. It wasn't even so much that we were just doing it for money, but there's got to be a reciprocal action. Everybody's gotta grow together. We had more demands, a lot more interviews, a lot more photos, more gigs and it just seemed like all this work for the same dick we were getting before. I distinctly remember Warner Bros picking us up off a plane from Europe as we were connecting to Australia and taking us in a limo across LAX [Los Angeles International Airport]. We sat there, got these gold records and took pictures with the executives and were then left to carry on as normal. We were still broke, except nobody believed it. We were like, 'What is this fuckin bullshit, taking a bunch o' pictures for a bunch o'monkeys!' We wanted to know where it all was? What about us? We didn't know anything about how the recording shit works."

"It was absolutely frustrating," agrees Bottum, "we'd toured for two years and things became a big bummer. We stopped at LAX and took pictures with these people for our gold or platinum record, 'Look we got our record.' And our record company's there pattin' us on the back before they all suddenly vanish! We have a 50 million hour flight to wherever, and it was *fucked*. I think that as long as any band is involved with management and record companies, you're gonna be fucked. People are out to get as much as they can out of you. Still to this day people treat us like that. They don't care if we're happy, they don't care if we're tired, they don't care how many shows on the road we have to play. And that's when it became most apparent to us that we were being used. People were making money from us who didn't care whether we were happy or not. And people are always pushing you as hard as they can to get their profits. It'll be that way until we stop doing whatever we're doing. People get their percentage and that's the bottom line."

It takes musicians a long time to get paid for their album sales, especially when your cheques are also going to the wrong Gould. For a while, Gould's publishing cheques were being sent to a registered writer 'Barbara Gould', which only served to make things seem even worse than they really were.

GOULD: "Our only Rolling Stone story came out around then, and all we did was bitch about how much money we weren't getting. But to us, and this is really important, for the kind of band we are and where we were coming from, the only other band who'd been through this was the Beastie Boys. We went in to a major label as a major experiment. We went in with the intention that we could handle our situation. All our tours were independently run, there was an indie scene still going on and none of our peers were considering making that change. There's the old story everybody grows up with, 'one of the reasons I've always been into indie labels is that major labels suck, they completely control the content of what the artist puts out and they end up ripping the artist off anyway.' It's the story everybody grows up with, the big label that fucks the little guy over.

"So we went in with this story ringing in our ears, but I was sick of making what I thought was good music and not having any money. It's like people telling you that masturbation makes you blind: 'Great fuck it, I wanna do it anyway *prove* it to me.' So we went in with this attitude of, 'fuck us, let's see if you fuck us.' So when we got this platinum record after all this work with nothing coming back, we were really cynical. We thought it had happened to us, that we'd been fucked. Our first reaction was, 'They've got us and now they're trying to bleed us.' Like the whole 'gold album photo thing' at LAX. I mean, what the fuck was that all about? It had nothing to do with us, that's for sure. Now, for a White Lion maybe that's how it works. I'm not knocking them, I'm just saying that's consistent with their game, but we're not from that background. Our response is, 'what the fuck are you doing with us and how are you exploiting us you scumbag pieces of shit! What do we get out of this, we see what *you* get out of it.' We're the guys who fuck up every night and eat it! I was more pissed off at

Warren, because our management is who we trust and we were left wondering if they were lying to us. They weren't, but we didn't know. We were paranoid to begin with."

An altogether more dangerous and aggravating situation was about to go beyond Gould, Bottum, Bordin and Martin's control. Mike Patton was realizing that he didn't particularly enjoy being the world's pin-up kid and, what's more, he didn't have to take it. Bungle still beckoned from Eureka, and with Faith No More suddenly the household name, perhaps Mike Patton had a developing option. It was still a hard one to understand, however inevitable, when Patton started playing Mr Bungle off against Faith No More and making them sweat. There was no apparent 'why'.

"When 'success' comes, you don't know it's going to happen it just does," spits Patton, "you're not 'prepared'. You may think you'd be comfortable dying tomorrow, but you don't really know. But for me, not only was I unprepared but I didn't give a fucking shit. To me, this little movie was going to have a happy ending or a bad ending. It was completely beyond my control and I would just have to wait and see."

There was a point in time when Patton realized that his mental scenario of Faith No More as school was not going to work out quite that way.

"When I came to grips with my lack of control over any of that stuff, I realized my plan wouldn't quite happen like I wanted it to. I think it was the same for any of us. Being in a band is like being in your own empire of five people: each of you vote on having this or that happen, and there are no other powers. Whether or not you got along in society you still had your own little government, even though it didn't matter. And then there was the fact that Faith No More wasn't like my other musical experiences, inbred, cuccoon-like, it wasn't imploding it was *exploding*. It made no sense to me. There were so many people involved in ways that I had no comprehension they could be. I think the further that you get in bullshit, the more it grates. When you feel it around your ankles it's not so bad. Then you start to smell it around your waist. And it hits you, ' Fuckin' wait a minute, I'm sinking!'"

The travelling was a major factor in wearing Patton down on that endless tour. Making things worse was his emergence as an '80's poster boy, who's ability became strictly secondary to his appearance.

" Yeah, that 'responsibility' of being the major factor in selling a million albums. Carry *that* one on my back! Pah! But once again, by lowering your standards and eating a little bit of shit you develop a taste for it. You think, 'There's no way I'm ever gonna ever change the way any of this happened, the way anybody listens to our music, the reasons why people picked up our album.' And I really don't care why anybody listens to our music, or picks up our album. If they look at our pictures, if they like the little logo, if they like the colours, if it's astrologically correct, if it's politically correct it doesn't matter, I don't *give* a shit. It's not going to make me feel any better, or any of us feel any better, if people are listening to our music 'for the right reasons'. There is no 'right reason'. It's no worse to be twelve years old and latch onto music than it is to be a fuckin' critic who says, 'listen to this it's cool.' Nobody's into music for the ight reason. Music overall is sometimes a pretty bad idea, an awful thing!

Those glib sentiments and feelings inside Mike Patton undoubtably lead to the fulfilment of his Mr Bungle project, regardless of the emotional cost to members of Faith No More. They were left to sit and listen to Patton extol the virtues of Bungle in the world's press, all the while insulting his 'working' bandmates.

AUTHOR'S INTERLUDE #4

I remember clearly thinking what total and utter bullshit it was that Mike Patton would shamelessly use Faith No More to vault his other band. He seemed hellbent on insulting them in interviews whenever possible (calling them 'old men' and so on) and promoted Bungle to a sickening degree whilst on FNM duty. You'd never have thought he had it in him, this cheery-faced, happy-go-lucky innocent in his suburban white-boy hip-hop gear and big basketball boots. He seemed so harmless, so incapable of fucking anyone. I mean Jeezuz, he didn't drink alcohol, choosing to extol the virtues of soda-pop, and freely talked with the western world about his love of masturbation and porno. He was, in every cliched sense, a teenager on the loose buying porno and soda pop. He talked stupid shit without really knowing much about anything. And what's more, he enjoyed the reaction! I'd ask him why, and he'd just look me right in the eye, cheeky smirk creeping across his face, and say, "Because of people like YOU! HAHAHAHAHA!"

I went out of my way to avoid talking about, or talking to, Mr Bungle at that time. I turned down 3 or 4 assignments because I couldn't stand what the fucking guy was doing. Obviously a talented and clever person, Patton was behaving like a total brat, an arsehole and it just seemed unfair that a band who had done nothing to punish him should have to suffer the indignities Patton was putting them through. There again no-one within Faith No More was really talking that much to him. Both were still sniffing each other out, unsure of each other's motives, always thinking the worst of each other. Whilst Patton was into Magic Johnson and Bugs Bunny, Gould was into the cult of serial killers and mass murderers. Not a lot of bridging space for converation there I'm afraid.

No-one ever talked too much about Patton and Mr Bungle, about his bad-mouthing Faith No More and claiming Bungle was his 'main' interest. So he was free to roam the media-waves unchecked, spouting off at any opportunity. Patton is crystal clear as to why he handled the situation the way he did.
'People like you ya sonofabitch! *You* were the ones who didn't help. God I hated your guts man, HA HA HA. But in a way it was pleasing that people such as you reacted in that way. It was like I was punching and punching and punching and no-one was hitting back, and I was thinking, 'Hey what's going on? I want a reaction here.' It was pleasing to see people that were protective of the band, but God it made me sick! Everybody with this 'interest' in the band, like it was everyone's 'baby'. And I just wanted to fuck their baby in the ass.

'I mean, my position in the whole thing never entered into it. When it first came up, it wasn't a hostility thing, it wasn't some violent weapon that I was using this band as

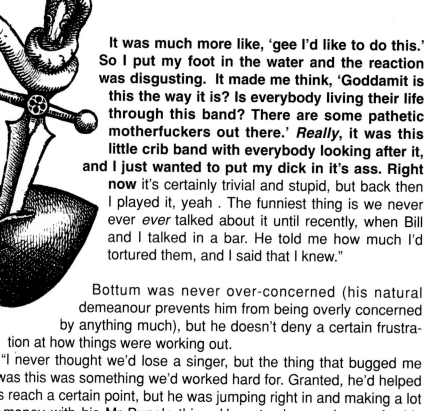

It was much more like, 'gee I'd like to do this.' So I put my foot in the water and the reaction was disgusting. It made me think, 'Goddamit is this the way it is? Is everybody living their life through this band? There are some pathetic motherfuckers out there.' *Really*, it was this little crib band with everybody looking after it, and I just wanted to put my dick in it's ass. **Right now** it's certainly trivial and stupid, but back then I played it, yeah . The funniest thing is we never ever *ever* talked about it until recently, when Bill and I talked in a bar. He told me how much I'd tortured them, and I said that I knew."

Bottum was never over-concerned (his natural demeanour prevents him from being overly concerned by anything much), but he doesn't deny a certain frustration at how things were working out.

"I never thought we'd lose a singer, but the thing that bugged me was this was something we'd worked hard for. Granted, he'd helped us reach a certain point, but he was jumping right in and making a lot of money with his Mr Bungle thing. He got a huge advance for his little 'side project' ($100,000) when the rest of the band had never used the band in that way. We'd never made money off side-projects in the blatant way he did. It was really aggravating that he would use us to make money for him and his friends. But at the same time it was still eggshells. We felt that if we brought it up to him, he'd just kinda flip and there'd be this huge scene that no-one wanted to deal with.

"We talked about it when it was going on, but with really padded gloves. I don't think anybody as being really honest about it. And I think that he probably said he enjoyed seeing us squirm over the whole thing, but I don't think he really did. To make yourself look good, you'd probably say that. But no-one was really squirming, and I don't think he'd seriously be that happy if people were. It doesn't seem like he's that type of person. I think he was just feeling really guilty and saying that to make himself feel and look a little better. Who would be happy making people squirm? I don't think he's that sort of person at all to tell you the truth. He wasn't sure what he was doing, whether it was right or wrong. And when he realized that what he was doing was brash and borderline wrong, I think he kinda panicked."

The upshot of all the aggravation was that Patton, also handled by WEM, was backed into the corner of signing a deal with Reprise/WB Records. One thing which didn't go down so well, was the fact that Mr Bungle got a higher advance than Faith No More had ever received.

GOULD: "I was still living out of my suitcase. It was like a joke. And Patton poor guy, he went from nothing to platinum in a year and back to nothing. Because this platinum bullshit may make you cover boy hunk of the month, but it really means nothing. Then he's got this other thing from our area, 'Don't do this band.' But I was pissed off when he ended up with a better deal than us, I even got another ulcer I was so pissed! Our band *got* him that deal, he knew it, everybody knew it. At that point, with another singer-situation coming up, it just seemed like we were getting fucked from all sides by everybody. And we had bills, debts to pay." "

To cap it all off, at the Monsters Of Rock show which was travelling throughout Europe in August 1990, the troublesome Patton decided to toss a few insults at other musicians on the bill. Admittedly his comments were amusing, but they also endangered the immediate career of Faith No More. Egos at such levels are fragile, and Patton wasn't sweet-talking anyone. At one festival in Belgium, Patton proclaimed that Lenny Kravitz and Sinead O'Connor were having sex backstage, whilst in Bologna, Italy he loudly announced that the drummer from Poison could, 'suck his own dick'.

BOTTUM: "I guess there was this chicken shit sense of glee at the fact that it came from his mouth and we could all be happy, if I'd have been fronting a band at that point I wouldn't have said what he said. We defended him to some extent and stood up for him, on the other hand we weren't the ones who said it and took the flak for it."

"I was just alive, affirming that we are all alive,"

"I was just alive, affirming that we are all alive," shrugs Patton at the memory. "In those situations you [front-people] have a common thing. You're all on a string, you're all in a really awkward situation where you don't really feel comfortable but you'd admit it sometimes and that would be that. And then we had our own feeling towards these things. Instead of being honourable and saying, 'thanks but no thanks,' or rather than having a good attitude about those shows and tours like 'let's just try this' (which we had for the first couple of times), after a while it became, 'Oh no'. We *had* to do it, we couldn't say no. So it became a case of, 'let's just make it as hard as we can for ourselves and everyone else.' And no-one else cares about your 'guilt' at doing those shows. No-one else wants to hear, 'I'm sorry we're here'. It's self-defeating; if you're sorry then don't do it in the first place. That's the only way this band is going to die, by our own hands because of stuff like that."

Faith No More were the hottest band in America. 'The Real Thing' was a steady top twenty album and 'Epic' was a top five smash-hit. Europe had been in love with them for a few years now, so when the chance to support Billy Idol came up in September, it was questionable who was going to benefit more from the bill. Idol was not quite the force he once had been, and night after night many of the people in the audience were there to see Faith No More and Mike Patton come to life after months of MTV play-back. It was yet more confusion for the spinning member's heads, but at least there was light at the end of the financial tunnel.

GOULD: "It was the Billy Idol tour when we finally got some money, an advance on our royalties. I remember sitting in a hotel in Portland at the restaurant, watching all these businessmen in suits eating their lunches and thinking, 'I can eat anything those guys are eating.' And

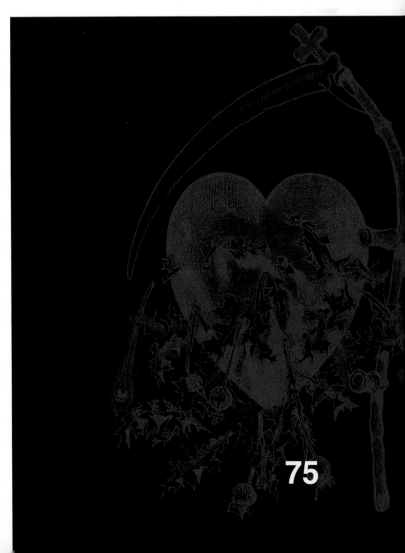

75

that was a very big thing to me. *That* was the real thing to me at that time. Eating well, being able to take a cab."

"I think we really kinda earned that tour more than the Metallica one, which was kind of a gift from those boys," sighs Martin, " At the time of Billy Idol we were on auto-pilot for sure, but it was still fun. He had a good attitude towards us, sort of, 'do what the fuck you want, talk shit if you can it doesn't matter.'"

BOTTUM: "Well, I think it would've been a lot more rewarding. That's the best a record ever did for us was during the Billy Idol tour. On our own tour, we'd have felt the rewards a lot more, the effects of being on the road, of people being into our band and being there to see our music. On the Idol tour it was confusing. We didn't know who was there to see us because we were opening up. It was very unclear as to who was there to see us and who was there to see him. We seemed to go down *really* well but nonetheless..."

It was the the tour that threw open the circus element of rock stardom.
GOULD: "Yeah, like going out with The Ringling Bros Barnum And Bailey, little kids with popcorn and shit. We were thinking, 'What the fuck is going on? This isn't cool.'
BOTTUM: "For some reason that tour just seemed really 'camp'. Even Billy Idol had a good sense of humour about what he was doing. I mean his stigma and his whole schtick onstage was *very* campy, *very* tongue-in-cheek, so in that sense I was a lot more comfortable on that tour than some of the others we've done. Guns N'Roses, Metallica, bands like that have a very hard time laughing at themselves."

Patton was finally coming down from his lofty and irritating position, realizing that matters weren't going to change. He was understanding that he couldn't reverse the magazine covers or the fame or the screams in his ear. He de-sensitized. He started not getting involved in trying to decipher the genuine compliments from the slew of brow-nose gibberish laid upon the band by all manner of assholes.
"You can't take time to 'screen' the genuine people from the fake. Everything is one big quagmire, and you become much more defensive about everything. I mean, you have to trust the people in your own camp, unless you wanna be like Jello Biafra. You can't be like that, so you have to adopt certain measures. First of all, you can go along with the program: you're a musician, you'll be in your place, you'll spend all your money and be an idiot, have, all these cars in the garage, sell no more records, your life will be over and you'll commit suicide. Or you can go to the other extreme: this is all bullshit, everything's bullshit, I hate music, I hate people, I'm gonna sit in my room and play my Lowrey organ for the rest of my life. Which makes you just as much of an idiot. So you have to find middle ground in order to survive."

There was to be one final mini-tour in the US with Robert Plant.
"We earned the Robert Plant tour as well," remembers Martin, "he always has his feelers out listening for musical trends and bands, and I guess he liked us. It was a very enjoyable tour, we were touring with Plant who is somewhat legendary, and the tour was in the old West USA in towns like Larramee, Wyoming. Plant was pretty much the same way as Billy Idol, in

as much as he would also encourage us to talk as much shit as we could get away with and have a good time. I really enjoyed that tour."

The year ended with Faith No More as the critics favourite (American magazines Spin, Rip and Canada's Music Express magazines named them the 'band of the year') and the people's choice. They headlined that year's Rip Magazine Anniversary show at the Hollywood Palladium, performing their cover of Black Sabbath classic 'War Pigs', with Ozzy Osbourne appearing as the guest vocalist. Just in case anybody got the impression this was a one-dimensional band, they then jammed with rapper Young MC. Faith No More appeared to be on the brink of enormous, sustained and steady success.

AUTHOR'S INTERLUDE #5

1991

Meeting up at Los Angeles International Airport, there was a sense of huge excitement at going to Rio De Janiero, Brazil for the world's biggest music festival. It was January, and the second 'Rock In Rio' to take place, 12 days of music to be played out at the huge 140,000 capacity Maracana Stadium. Faith No More were to appear under Guns N' Roses and Billy Idol as the headliner's first-night special guests. Reportedly Axl Rose had requested they be on the same night as G N'R, not an enormous surprise as Rose was a very vocal supporter of the band. And here we all were on the same Varig flight going to Rio, Rose sitting across from the band checking out a wide selection of CD's, Faith No More seat-swapping and bullshitting with each other the whole way.

It was crazy from start to finish. The band couldn't leave the hotel without being mobbed by fans, and as they were enjoying the powerful shove of MTV, there was always a camera crew going everywhere. One night we all crammed into two tiny VW campers, MTV wanting to take the band to a Samba school. The vehicles were immediately surrounded by fans, climbing all over them, pounding the roof, beating the glass, trying to pry open locked doors. Hot breath fogged in the windows as faces peered in, screaming, yelling, beating, pounding. Total immersion. Claustrophobia. Gould started screaming and yelling back, hammering the inside of the van in imitable fashion of the fan's fists outside. this egged them on. Finally we took off, captured our breath and headed for a samba night somewhere.

The van broke down in a desolate area of Rio. We stood around for about an hour, told not to wander too far as the streets out here were dangerous. We missed the Samba, but headed for this tiny rock club, where we sat and started to get bored before Prince showed up plus about six bodyguards. Roddy led us over to his table, where he tried striking up conversation with the purple one. No go. A slight nod here, an odd look there, communication was minimal and Prince looked enormously silly, like he was on (and from) another planet. Maybe he is. Even his six bodyguards looked embarrassed.

Billy wanted to find a 'Macumba' ritual chicken sacrificing, but the promoter's liaison wouldn't help him. 'You have a show to do, until then I cannot let you endanger yourself,' was all he would say. Then MTV took everyone wind-sailing high off a famous cliff above the Ipanema

Beach. Yet none of it seemed as exciting as the band's show. Patton was sporting his new 'short' hair cut for the first time. His innocence was gone with the rest of his locks, his whole demeanour now more sinister, more violent. The show was incredible, an hour which should've been two and 130,000 people going crazy as the dusk fell. Puffy was a maniac behind the drums, Gould was throwing his life into the show, Bottum was more dramatically involved than I'd ever seen him, Martin's legs were straddled, head swinging, hair flying, glasses clinging on for dear life. And Patton was re-born. No longer nice, no longer friendly, Rock In Rio was the first manifestation of his more violent and physical stage demeanour. Even Slash, the G N'R guitarist standing at the side of the stage, was shakin' his ass like his life depended on it. It surpassed any show Faith No More had ever done.

If there was to come a point at which Faith No More started to drift apart from itself, then the Rock In Rio appearance in Brazil was when it began, and that September's tour of South America and Japan was it's maturation.

"At Rock In Rio suddenly personalities and egos come out," says Martin, "just down to the fact that loads of people show up at the the hotel everyday and shout and yell at whoever comes out. Some people took it personally. I think that also happened on our month-long South American tour, where people would be at the hotels and some folk started thinking maybe they were as 'great' as the people were shouting they were."

Gould has an entirely different recollection of both Rock In Rio and the South American/Japanese tour .

" Everything about it *was* great. Most bands that went to Rock In Rio complained about it, but for us everything was really cool. So we went back down to South America, and Brazil in particular, for a month-long tour. It was two years of constant, hard roadwork at that point. But to the average guy it's a case of, 'what the fuck have those guys been up to?' We hadn't even had a chance to get into writing 'Angel Dust'."

Most of 1991 was about writing the follow-up to a smash-hit album. There was, of course, pressure but no-one's too keen to admit it. The rift between Martin and the band started getting even stronger, each disagreing about the other's input in terms of amount and quality. But one thing had eventually happened. Mike Patton had, suddenly and inexplicably, become an integrated part of the writing team.

PATTON: "I never knew what kind of band it was. We became a hard rock band by default, it was an accident, but the beautiful thing was that we all knew. We could look at each other and say however bad it got, however much of a pet monkey we became, however much of a pet funk-metal rock band we were, there were 4 other guys who have to deal with it to. And each guy dealt with it in their own little way. There had never been any question of my staying in the band. We started writing the music for this album, and being a part of something so fundamental was what made sure of it for me. 'The Real Thing' had been like someone else's music, someone else's band, it had felt like an obligatory thing. They hadn't *needed* a damn singer, it was just that they had to have a singer. That's why I was there, that's why Chuck was there, we weren't needed we were there.

"Before this album I still threw ideas out, whether that be fool's courage or whatever, so I

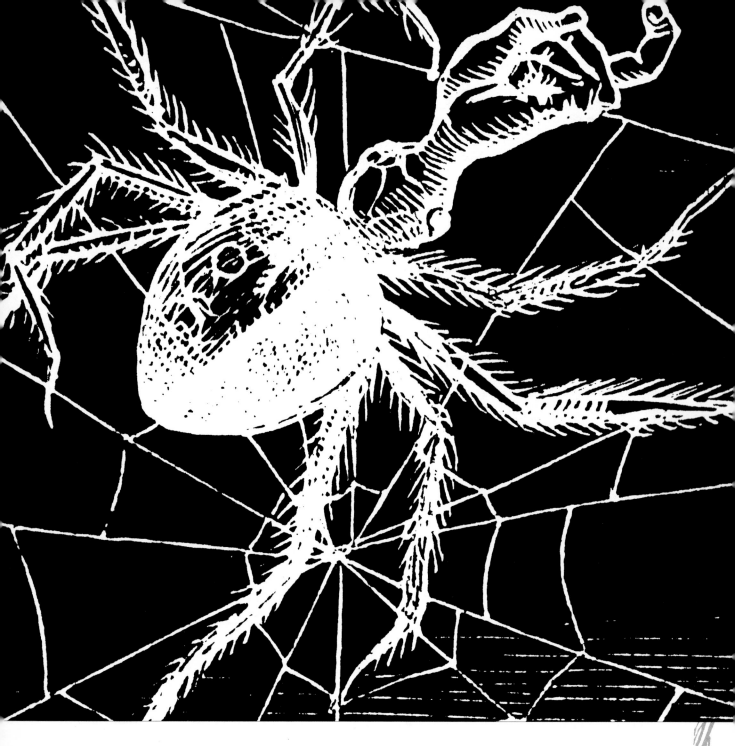

always had the courage. It was just the fact we started from the pot in the middle where everybody pees into it. We'd done our time, so it felt like we'd been in jail with someone for a while. Like a junkie, it doesn't matter whether you agree with someone's way of thought, what they do for a living or what they do in their spare time, it doesn't matter because whatever it was you were there. Proximity made it happen. And now, of course, we're kinda friends in a weird sort of way."

Matt Wallace has been aware of the creative tension that Faith No More creates from the very beginning, recognizing that things would never be easy with them in a studio. "As far a tension goes, they use it to it's utmost to where they get their best results and that's unique. They're also the only band I've worked with who is a true democracy. If any one person came out and said 'I'm in charge,' everyone else would say 'fuck *you* , what are *you* sayin?' Which is great! And the fact that it's five people; you could never have a tie with them. It's like a spider web with these five lines going out where the web is pulling them together. And the strength of the web, is in the fact that all five are pulling equally out and away from the centre. On 'The Real Thing', Patton was into Sade, he loved Sade, and of course Martin was into Metallica and Black Sabbath, Bottum was into Marky Mark or whoever. They were all pulling in different directions equally, and that's the one thing I've always applauded about this band. If someone says, 'we're gonna do a really poppy song,' all the other guy are behind it. And if Martin wanted to do this really dirty fucked up metal thing all the guys would be there, they wouldn't say, 'oooh I'm into Sade I can't get into this metal stuff.' There was always a lot of exchange for all the obvious tension."

The 'Angel Dust' recording process had many different facets. On one hand there was the development of Mike Patton musically, on the other the disturbing rift between everyone and Jim Martin.

"I never sense this band bowing to any commercial and artistic guidelines imposed..."

WALLACE: "I think first of all that the record label, public, everyone wanted 'The Real Thing part 2' which would've been a safe bet. Much to their credit they didn't, and I never sense this band bowing to any commercial and artistic guidelines imposed. I think they wanted to exercise their freedom and make a challenging record. That hit everyone, we'd all hit points where we thought 'piece of shit'. There were many times when there was confusion and near-paranoia. They'd call me and I'd tell them it would be fine. Bordin would be on the phone, then he'd be fine, then it'd be Bill, then someone else. Then I'd wonder about it myself, so we all had periods of doubt. It was that old thing of everyone knowing what they didn't want to do but not really being sure of what they wanted. Patton was incredibly prepared. He hadn't quite finished the lyrics on the demos and I remember thinking what a lazy fuck he was, but then as we progressed I realized he had four completely different versions of the lyrics for certain songs, each one taking things to another place. That's when I knew he was taking this really seriously, and many times we'd discuss his agonizing over a word or phrase. Patton was right there at all stages of the musical process."

It was also the completion of Patton's self-reinvention, to dark and twisted from bright, youthful and bubbly.
WALLACE:"As much as Patton may well have reinvented himself because of all the 'teen stuff' that happened before, the whole 'pop good looking young guy' person, neither is really him. He's probably somewhere in the middle. But that 'Real Thing' stuff was certainly a lot for him, confronting all that celebritism of being adored. Even when women offered themselves to him sexually he'd say, 'What is that about? You don't know me why would you wanna do that?' I've always admired that about him, he's honest. Patton saying he'd rather masturbate than have sex with a woman he hardly knows is brilliant! You wouldn't hear Warrant or Motley Crue have the balls to say that crap. So now Patton's journey is leading him to the darker, doomier stuff and maybe now he feels confident enough to lean back into the band and have a good response."

Wallace is unequivocally clear on just how hard the album was.
"I have to say that the whole album was horrible to work on from the start. Patton was trying a lot of these weird things, which took us all a bit to get used to, and Jim wasn't completing his parts. I don't know why that was. The band had always rehearsed in San Francisco, and Jim asks if they could rehearse in the East Bay and split the commute a little more evenly. So the four guys drive across the bridge from San Francisco to Oakland and he rarely

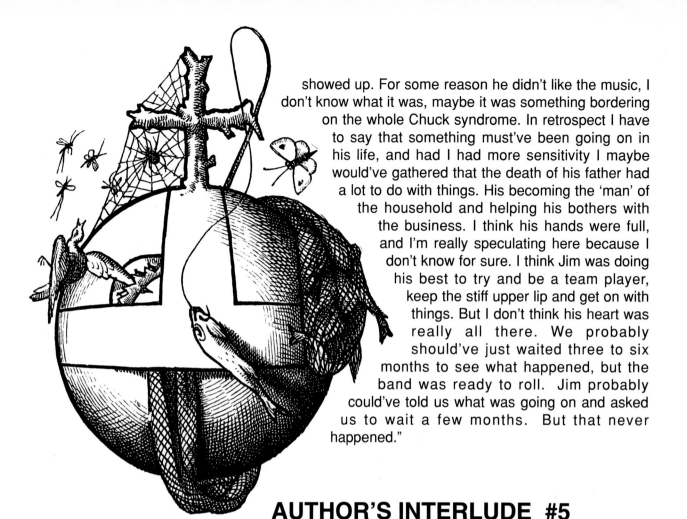

showed up. For some reason he didn't like the music, I don't know what it was, maybe it was something bordering on the whole Chuck syndrome. In retrospect I have to say that something must've been going on in his life, and had I had more sensitivity I maybe would've gathered that the death of his father had a lot to do with things. His becoming the 'man' of the household and helping his bothers with the business. I think his hands were full, and I'm really speculating here because I don't know for sure. I think Jim was doing his best to try and be a team player, keep the stiff upper lip and get on with things. But I don't think his heart was really all there. We probably should've just waited three to six months to see what happened, but the band was ready to roll. Jim probably could've told us what was going on and asked us to wait a few months. But that never happened."

AUTHOR'S INTERLUDE #5

I spoke to Bill Gould in the December of 1991, interested in how the album was coming along. He had a tape of the rough tracks and was half-willing to let me hear them, repeating over and over that 'they were rough tracks and not to read anything into them'. Like all Faith No More songs, they grew and grew as I listened to the tape a couple of times. Gould remained impassive, sitting on the floor grumbling here and there, remarking on where a 'guitar part' was going to be. I asked him why the part wasn't in yet and he said that Jim was slacking off, not coming up with stuff. In a couple of instances, Bill showed me where he'd filled in some guitar crap just to give the tape some shape. It was the first I knew of any real problems between the band and Jim. I'd always thought, much like everyone else, that this creative 'tension' stuff was par for the course. Bill was stressing heavily and I repeated to him that it seemed this was just the way the band worked, to the outsider it was how their albums got done. Bill would have none of it. He told me, repeatedly, that this was more serious than all that, that Jim wasn't plugged in and didn't care to be. I asked Jim later what he thought of the songs, and he said that for the most part he didn't like them, thought that the band were 'trying too hard' instead of throwing caution to the wind and letting stuff happen as it would. I remember at first sympathizing solely with him, feeling that the band didn't understand Martin once more, thinking that he was being scapegoated. It wasn't nearly that simple.

WALLACE: "The rows between Bill and Jim started with the demos, where it was obvious that the parts weren't right and we had to work on them. Bill had offered to work on parts with him. Jim had said he'd be fine doing them alone. I went to sit out at his place with him, working ideas and everything, and Jim either would not or could not get into it. So the

recording process was acrimonious from the start. In a couple of places the contributions were good, but for the most part they sounded watered down — did not have the meat 'n' potatoes, ballsy, fuck-you attitude that Jim brought to the Faith No More table. What he brought was always very important for the sound; he's heard and felt. He balances this band out. If he's not there, the Faith No More see-saw will balance into the artsy-craftsy pop music thing. When Jim's doing his best, he swings that massive club and there's crunch and raw power. That whole 'Ugly Jim Martin' which was so important, that whole 'fuck you' attitude wasn't there."

Big Sick Ugly Jim lives in all of us from time to time, something the mellow Wallace isn't afraid to acknowledge.
"All of us would love to have that attitude and be Jim Martin for a day—a man of few words, that Clint Eastwood 'Man With No Name.' This Jim Martin of the past, where he could say, 'Fuck you,' and where he was bluntly honest. He'd tell you exactly how he felt, and I admired that in him. No beating around the bush; if it sucked, he'd tell you straight. We missed that on 'Angel Dust' from Jim Martin, and while he did say certain things about the music, we didn't agree with him. He didn't write any songs except for 'Jizzlobber,' and usually Jim brings a number of ideas to the table. So the acrimony was high. We'd record his stuff at night and we'd talk. I'd tell him that what he was playing sounded wimpy. That it didn't have the backbone we needed. He said he heard light melodic songs, which made him play light melodic things. These melodious one-line things, and I wanted to know where the fuckin' crunching stuff was. The next morning, Bill, Roddy and Patton would show up to hear what Jim had done and I would just play them the stuff. Invariably they'd all get up and stomp around the room yelling, 'What the fuck is *that*? What the hell is he *doing* to our record?' Patton was very very vocal about it, Bordin would then chime in, and Roddy was pretty easy-going, but it got to the point where even he was wondering what was up. They'd have these meetings with Jim: 'Hey what's goin' on here,' and nothing would ever come out.

"On a personal note, 'Angel Dust' was one of the most difficult records I've ever worked on in my life. The difficulties between Jim and the band, coupled with the fact that the support team behind the studio [Coast Recorders] was horrible, it all wore me out to the point where I had to take 3 months off. If I'd have done one more thing I'd have quit the business. But looking back, it turned out to be a fabulous record ."

To further illustrate the tensions during 'Angel Dust's creation, there follows the full transcript of an interview conducted by the author for a Kerrang! magazine article during February 1992 at Coast Recorders in San Francisco. At the time 'Angel Dust' was nearing the mix stage.

"There will be no middle ground for this album," stated Bill Gould, "it's either gonna be absolutely huge or it'll bomb wildly, be a total fucking flop."

Faith No More are just mixing their fourth album, titled 'Angel Dust', and already the walls are stretching to contain it's occupants. The whole lot of 'em are fretting over nothing, Jim Martin's been in the doghouse since before Christmas and but for the fact Faith No More is a democracy certain ideas would've hit the toilet ages ago. The inner-turmoil that the band have been eager to dismiss as 'media-hype' in the past is a huge dirty-great fact, inescapable and intrinsic to Faith No More's work. They need to piss each other off and manage to achieve this act in some fine fashion consistently.

I first of all asked them about the pressure involved following up a hugely successful album?

BOTTUM: "Everyone's pretty much left us alone,I think it was from ourselves more than anybody. The record company and management were worried about just what we were going to do, but they kept their worries from us. "

GOULD: "In the past we've always stuck together because we were totally broke and we needed to put out another album for the union scale money, after this last tour we just split and went our separate ways, so we haven't been in any real rush to get back together.

...en you come to putting the material ...ether for this album, you obviously ...d to go as diversely opposite to what ...'re expected as possible.

Part of the pressure in the past was economic adversity, being stuck with these people and knowing you had to stick with them because it was your only way out. When you take that incentive away you realize that there's a chemistry there because you've always got something out of it and it's trying to tap into it."

BOTTUM: "We all knew specifically what we wanted to avoid, the whole 'funk-metal' thing, it was very obvious that nobody wanted to follow those lines. Pressure's if you hear something in your head and you're not getting it when you're writing it or recording it, making the pieces of the puzzle fit. That's the kind of pressure we're under. Theres no pressure in the style you adopt, but if you're not getting your ideas right sometimes that's when it becomes pressure. You think you've lost your ability to arrange things properly so as they fit in the right order."

Do you find yourselves sitting around wondering just how the hell this whole thing took off like it did last time out?

Roddy: "No, I mean touring as long as we did left us with plenty of time to realize how it was happening and why, to think about it and deal with it."

When you come to putting the material together for this album, you obviously tend to go as diversely opposite to what you're expected as possible.

'I don't know if you can think about it like that," says the fired-up little Gould, "you just get sick of doing something for a year-and-a-half, and reading...look, even if you don't pay attention to what they say this whole 'funk-metal' thing is really disgusting. The last thing I ever want to be in is a funk-metal band, so it's not like we're gonna try

...to go the exact opposite but anything except that y'know.
People will want to hear those old songs live still.
"But those are just songs. They're NOT funk metal, fuck that! It's just a disgusting label for a band, and I would say that any band which plays funk-metal I hate. I would safely say that most of the band feels the same way."

So, the new material...you have songs which sound like sleazy '70's cop shows and songs that'd strip the flesh of a dog's back from 1000 yards, so where's it all coming from? How much is Patton involved in all this? Quite a lot from what I gather...
GOULD: "Yeah he's way-involved, a lot more than the last record, he's handling pretty much all the lyrics and he's into it."
You don't like admitting that friction makes the whole thing work, but there we were again with you lot, another pissy-frontman dicking you around and yet it all clicked into gear and started to work just fine. So surely you can see that you need the tension.
"We go through a major bad trauma twice, at least once anyway, a week! hahahahaha..."
What was this week's Bill?
"The album cover was one, we got this fax saying we might have had to pay $20,000 for the sleeve until we found out we wouldn't have. But in the meantime we got our own pictures from someone we knew and rid it ourselves [the front cover is a fantastic shot of a heron in mid-rise on a lake of sorts, the back a bunch of meat-hooks with dead carcasses and a cow's head hanging - SC]..."

You've done the 'scummy-van route' so how much have you changed now that you're a rock star?
"Luckily I found the Lord Jesus Christ, and I've put all those drug-type of evils behind me...hahahaha. I discovered the Lord when I saw other bands more successful than Faith No More...NO SERIOUSLY, being successful is actually pretty good. I wouldn't know about whether I've changed or not, whether people around me think I've changed or not because I live in a Chinese neighbourhood where no-one speaks English. When they see me walking down the street they could be talking a lotta shit and I wouldn't know, hahaha."
Gould's landlord however, on hearing that the band were big rich famous rock stars, upped his rent a good 30%.
"That's true yes, but I'm gonna pour cement down the drains when I leave. But what's a mere 30% after all the millions and millions of dollars I made last year, a cheap price to pay HAHAHAHA..."
It's Bill's round I announce in reaction to his last comment.

So when it comes to Patton's lyrics do you get involved, do you want to know what he's writing about?
"We pretty much leave it to him," says Roddy, "I mean that's his job in the band, everyone has their input and words are his."
Bill: "He's really into his words, and as long as he's into them..."
You don't care.
Roddy: "No I do care, I care what he sings about sure but he's probably gonna get a lot o' flak this time around for what he's singing about, he's gonna offend a lot of people and I think it's great."
Such as.
"Well, there's a lot of things he's doing in character, which I think is really a cool thing, he likes to capture characters in his song. There's this one song about a white trash kinda trailer park person who's really repulsive y'know? But that whole angle is good, it's a really good angle to follow. I think if singers wanna do something like that then they should be able to, in the same way that actors who take on really sleazy roles don't get shit for it, don't get

Gould: "Child-molester."
Roddy: "I think a singer is along the same lines. People shouldn't take what singer's say so seriously, it shouldn't always be taken verbatim."

But then the more it offends the better it is in reality right?
"Keep that machine going!" laughs Gould.
"Well not even offensive, it's just good to stretch things to extremes," affirms Roddy. I ask him what other songs could be considered as 'stretching' and 'offensive'?
"Well I wrote some good lyrics for him on one song which he'll probably get some flak for called 'I Swallow' [later titled 'be Aggressive], it's about swallowing..."
About swallowing?
"Yeah...cum."
From any particular angle?
"Well...probably down on his knees I guess!"

Time to cough. Did you say Patton wrote those lyrics Roddy?
"No I wrote the words."
Oh so he's just going to be seen as the one who wrote them...
"Well there's a day of reckoning for every..."
OK, what is this exactly, is it standing up for gay rights?
"Not really, it's just more along the lines of the character thing, not even about offending anyone just about trying out different characters and being challenging."

So how has the writing come together, have you found that you've been bitching at each other like you always do?
"Some things are easier than before," says Bill, "...actually it was a lot harder when I think about it."
"Jim's getting a lot more comfortable with the songs now," furthers Roddy, "he's uncomfortable rehearsing the songs with us and he'd rather have a tape of the finished product and work on it at home, he likes separating and doing it by himself."

Bill: "It makes for a weird tension because even though he's working on his stuff at home, you visualize everything including the guitar when you write the song. And then it comes back different to your perception, but if the person isn't there from day one then they can't be expected to read your mind."
It just seems like you lot always bicker on like grannies at the bus stop. You assholes!
"Yeah, it's just another manifestation of the same old story. But we won't really know much more until the record's done and out, it'll all work out though..."

Matt Wallace later, and drunkenly, declares Jim 'the Puffy of the '90's'. Strong words indeed, fighting words to die for and Jim's response?
"I was the one who fuckin' said that one day because everybody was talking so much shit, but basically I cannot agree with that comment for real. If I am 'the Puffy of the '90's', then the definition's have got to change."

Jim. Grouchy old man. It seemed only fitting to allow him his chance to comment. First off, has it been a pleasant experience this album?

"Absolutely not, it's been an unpleasant experience from the very beginning. It's been very unpleasant, not really much different than my experience in making records with Faith No More before, I mean, it's always been a very unpleasant experience. A lot of people scrambling to get henchmen on their side to play silly games, to blow smoke on a situation, to diffuse situations...it's very difficult to say it all in a short amount of time. There's certain things that certain people worry about at certain times. And certain other people know this and chose to play upon it to increase the tension of a given situation, letting the person feel that everything's way out of hand further than they could ever figure. Amplifying situations that do not exist, manipulating others..."

GIRLS ARE OK, BUT THEY'RE NOT

THE REAL THING

But hasn't that always been the way Jim?

"More than ever more than ever now."

Is it pressure showing itself?

"I'm not sure if it's that or more of one's desire to be a teen idol. Things really don't seem that much different than ever, except for the fact it's a little worse because certain members of the band seem worried."

You're not worried about things though right?

"No, not at this point. I was at one point, there was a problem because everyone seemed so frightened that I wondered it we'd be able to do anything. At this point there's no worry on my part at all."

"I think our egos have caught up with us now.."

How is it that you don't work with the rest of the band in person when writing and rehearsing [recording's different, Martin going in sharp at 10 am?

"Because usually I have to drive a long way, and I get there, and we'll play something when all of a sudden someone decides they wanna leave. Or somebody decides they're not having a nice day or whatever, they decide they wanna blow it off and I've driven all that way to go there. I dunno...I'm not too agreeable to begin with so that stokes the flames up a bit."

When you do something different musically then the bricks come tumbling right?

"I think that's mostly Bill's fault because it's like somehow somebody gets Bill to think something's wrong. I dunno how, and Bill's like the figurehead because he's always willing to say something, so if someone can get Bill going then they've got a good shot at having something played a certain way. There's where the whole thing about Bill being played like a violin and so forth comes in. I mean, I'm not trying to do anything different. I'm just trying to play these songs the way I see 'em the way it should go. It's not like we're trying to do anything 'different' we're not reinventing ourselves I'll tell ya that, we're going along as we can. Anything we play will pretty much sound like us if y'know what I mean, so don't let any of that 'doing something new' bullshit creep in because that's a load of fucking crap!"

Without this pushing and shoving though, Faith No More would really cease to exist right?

"I dunno man, I guess so...it's the nature of the beast. As long as these people are around that's the way it is. Some people are spoiled filthy little brats, rich parents, been handed everything on a golden platter..."

Be careful Jim, they could just as easily sling mud back at you.

"That's bullshit! Anybody can say anything, anybody can sling shit at anybody they want! What's the point of doing the interview?! Come on guy! But it's pretty much that guys sometimes act like spoilt children, and this is an industry and a job that encourages and permits that sort of behaviour."

Faith No More, monkeys trapped in a cage with each other, slinging shit all over the place.

The passage of change for Faith No More, from those early days in dive San Francisco bars with revolving singers, to the internationally acclaimed band making 'Angel Dust', was enormous. To move from the heart of alternativisim to the bosom of mainstream America without sacrificing yourself in the process, is a remarkable achievement.

BOTTUM: "Well, we've worked with our management a quite a long time, and it came to a point where we finally did trust them with things we'd always taken care of ourselves. Setting up the tours, making decisions on hotels we wanted to say in but there are still people we deal with who we don't entirely trust. I think that's always the way in any walk of life. Like when it comes down to T-shirt designs, I think we're best left to our own devices coming up

with T-shirt designs. If we were a typical band, I think we would let the T-shirt company come up with their own designs and pick and chose from what they came up with. As far as products go, I think it's pretty important to be hands-on. With record sleeves, T-shirts, advertising, we pretty much get the final say. It would be easier to let go of it all and allow people to take charge of absolutely 100% of everything but that would be an ugly scenario. But, of course, you have to know when to draw the line over what you will, and won't, handle."

In February 1991, Faith No More won five awards at the 14th Annual Bay Area Music Awards, The Bammies, in San Francisco. The band didn't appear to care one way or another though, stuck as they were in trying to write another album. Not even Martin's appearance in the Hollywood comedy sequel 'Bill And Ted's Bogus Journey', and a band cut on the soundtrack album, could revive the ailing sense of camaraderie between Martin and the rest of the band. He continued to seem disinterested in the music he was being asked to work with, and the band seemed increasingly aggravated by the state of affairs.

1992

When 'Angel Dust' was released, it was viewed as a daring left-field move by pretty much everybody who heard it. From the inside, though, that wasn't so.

BOTTUM: "I don't think the music has changed that much at all. In the early days we'd get onstage and do these repetitive, looping riffs over and over . We just thought that the repetitiveness and heaviness of that structure was so intense, just going over and over was so intense and so original that we were really cocky about what we were doing. And I talked to this guy recently who hadn't heard us since 'The Real Thing' who was designing a T-shirt for us. I remember saying to him 'pretty different huh?' about 'Angel Dust'. And he didn't think it was different more than it was pretty much the same. I sat back and thought about it and realized he was right. What we're doing today is pretty much the same, save the singer who puts things in a different light. But the structure of the music is the same, that repetitive heavy structure is still the main thing. And I think it's good that we've stuck to our roots, stuck with this one ethic.

"I think our egos have caught up with us now though, I wouldn't say we're as cocky as we were then. It's very easy when you're a band starting out to be absolutely cocky, because you have nothing to disprove that, we had no records out there to make things otherwise, so we could be as cocky as we wanted to be and get way with it. But now we have all this history behind us, so if we were to be cocky and conceited about what we're doing, people

could look back and say 'well this record isn't so great.' And I'd maybe agree with them. We've put out some pretty inferior things looking back. 'Introduce Yourself' when I re-heard it had a lot of great ideas but that's it and the songs didn't sound as good as they did when we wrote them. I listen back to the vocals on that record and can't believe we put up with them at that point. They're unique, but with us effectively then putting out a Warner Bros album, it was pretty brash and assuming of us that people would appreciate his vocals the way they stood. I think at the time I saw Chuck as a much better singer than he was. "

MARTIN: "What I think right now, is that if you're in a group of people you might stand up and shout 'HEY'. Once everybody's paying attention, if you just carry on shouting 'hey hey hey' what kind of effect is that going to have? Everyone will stop paying attention to you, so you have to get on with it already. I think we need to start getting on with it. I think we have to carry on going forward, it's hard to say exactly what direction the band's moving in. A lot of people said this 'Angel Dust' record was different to the others, wheras to me it really wasn't. The only thing that's different are the vocals, and Mike Patton did the vocals differently on purpose to avoid the same as before."

From the album's completion, the band immediately stepped into the biggest tour in the world...and the biggest pile of shit they had yet trodden in!

got it! We can play to all these people who are just there for the event, and take 'em on board.' But it didn't translate like that. And it sucked! Guns N'Roses treated us very well, everything we needed we got and they made it as easy for us to tour as they could. We never saw them, but that was OK. For some reason though we hated it more than anything, hated the vibe, hated being around it. The thing about being on the biggest concert tour in the world is that it only exists because the biggest egos in the world want it to. It's like Napoleon, 'I want the biggest because it's fitting of my stature'. That vibe soaks through

every single bit of the **"Guns N'Roses treated us very well.."**
operation. I realized
early on that I hated Led
Zeppelin and the idea of what it meant; what's worse is when you're there and you can
actually see it for yourself. You suddenly have an educated opinion and you really hate it
more than ever, you can see the guy in the flesh and realize that it's all a stupid piece of shit.
It's no longer a gut feeling you have, it's an educated fact. I have a problem with it, and the
statement I'm about to make may sound pretentious itself but whatever. To see that the
things which influence our culture, such as music which is a tremendously big influence on
kids, are being driven by a machine out of control which is ignorant, self-servicing and has
nothing to do with why it existed in the first place, offends me. Because there are little kids
that grow-up and are succeptible to the media. Who don't have a choice and are fed this and
are given this shit by these self-serving pieces of shit. And then I go to places like eastern
Europe where I see people starving for it, starving for something.

"I'm guilty of it myself. I'll take the 'November Rain' video as an example. I'm not slagging the
guy off, but when I see Axl sitting at his piano or whatever, for some reason the photography,
the sound, the clothes they're wearing paints the picture of a well-educated, on top of it
lifestyle. It's a life that's real somewhere, and if I could ever meet this person I would be
'touched' by it. But those intentions were never there to begin with anyway, it's a sham,
you're being fucked because you're buying into this ugly myth. They're taking your money."
Of course, many people know exactly what dream they're buying when they go to a rock
show or buy an album or video. The fact is that many time, kids WANT their bands to carry
that falseness, that 'sophistication and poise. They want to believe that these are Gods
amongst men or women. That's why rock'n'roll is what it is, and if there's anything that Faith
No More may not yet have grasped properly, it is that whether they like it or not, they are
role-playing a variety of fantasies for millions of people. Just as Rose does. Just as all
famous musicians do.

Not understanding why the hell a band he'd done nothing but help were slagging him off in the international media circles, Axl Rose called a meeting in Miami.

GOULD: "We came to the show one day in Florida, and Warren and John were both there. I wondered why, and they said Doug Goldstein had told them they had to be there that day. So we're immediately thinking 'oh shit', we realized there was a serious problem. So I was in the dressing room playing guitar or something, when John asked if I could come out for a moment. And the band, Doug and Axl are all sitting around this table. Axl looks up at me and says, 'And you ya piece of shit, where d'ya get shittin' on me?' I guess he'd had about 7 or 8 magazines with us talking shit from the past 2 months thrust upon him. Our big thing was not to kiss his ass and play the game, if we were just to smile and take pictures of handshakes then what the fuck is that? I'd feel it was irresponsible, I'd feel it was far more responsible to say we never saw the guy. It's not good for your career but it's the truth. Patton said the worst shit, but Axl said 'you're a singer, you're temperamental and I understand that...but YOU,' pointing at me. I guess I was just a bass player ha ha ha.

"Roddy got off scot-free, Jim never had a problem with them in the first place because he's one of them, a rock guy who drinks, goes to the parties, etc and Puffy's a non-confrontation-alist. He said 'I wish they'd print all the good things I say about you guys in interviews,' so he washed his hands clean of the whole thing. We all went and apologized together, and to tell you the truth, he was cool. A couple of hours later he was hangin out, a likable guy. We actually felt bad that our mouths had got that out of control as to do the wrong thing. We thought we were doing the right thing, because we were offending people. And we're not used to that. We were always the scum-bags, the ones nobody gave a shit what we thought or said."

"It's fair to say those old feelings came out," winces Bottum at the memories, "when anyone's offered a chance to go out on a tour that big you kinda jump at the opportunity whether it's your crowd or not. You're playing to huge crowds of people and it's a challenge. We say 'yes' to pretty much everything that's offered to us, and when we say yes it doesn't seem like that big a deal. Then when we're out there doing it, things become totally different. And I guess it

just came down to us wanting to throw rocks at people. Of course, you can get away with it if you're on a high building, and people don't see you and you don't talk about it; you can hit a couple of people and have a good laugh. But we threw our rocks from the stage, out in the open, and people saw us doing it and we became perceived as the type of band that does that all the time.

"I think it bugged us that a lot people assumed we were joining 'their camp' and we wanted it to be absolutely clear that was not the case. We were also stuck in the awkward position as far as saying 'here we are but we're nothing like them.' And then the question of 'OK why did you join their tour', there was a real dichotomy there. Again here we were confusing the hell out of people, not sure what we're about. On the one hand we're saying 'we're all about G N'R, going on tour with these people and being this big rock thing,' and then there was the disproving of that, disproving that 'big rock thing'.

"And there's very few people like him [Axl Rose], there's very few people like that. You might say U2 but at least they have some validity, some political statement they're making, they're not all completely right-wing, they're not about the 'old school'. Like having strippers backstage, that whole scene y'know. It's absolutely outdated and never right in the first place. I mean groupies backstage and girls belittling women to this role of jumping around in scantily clad little outfits and being there at your disposal, and strippers backstage is just a hideous thing to me. Just reducing women to that level is really disgusting to me, it always has been and it's something we've never been about. I think that's what really turned me off, because we went to one of those parties after G N'R played and seeing the things they did after their show was really ugly. So unprogressive and I've always seen us as a progressive band in as much as being a forward thinking band, breaking boundaries as far as ethics go. Trying new things,

"everybody wants you to talk shit and you're like a goddam fish taking the bait.."

combining different aspects which don't usually go together, that's what we're about."

GOULD: "Our whole history is 'when in doubt, offend'. It was like having a big laugh, if we offended 90% of them and got 10% then that was who we were playing for. Then we reached a point where we realized if we offended people they would probably never buy our records again. It was a language we'd developed and a way we'd operated that we had to seriously re-evaluate, because it was becoming career-threatening. It was all just becoming ridiculous. It was good for us, because you do have to grow. Sit in the same habits all the time and you don't grow, but when we heard we were a Heavy Metal rock band the first thing we wanted to do was say that HM sucked. We wanted to say stuff like 'Axl might like us but we think that band's nothing but a piece of shit.' A lot of that is emotional reaction to things that are out of our control. It really had nothing to do with him, he was just a stool-pigeon and I know that isn't fair on him. But it wasn't an intellectual reaction, it was an emotional reaction."

Martin, of course, doesn't quite see the issue of offending Rose or anybody in this light.
"I remember people talking shit about others, and I don't really like it. Lots of times, in many circumstances, you're not much better, although the down-time was very tiresome and did lead to the shit-talking. There was so much time to waste, everybody wants you to talk shit and you're like a goddam fish taking the bait. All people have to do is dangle the clam and we'll bite. We're definitely responsible in certain circumstances, many times it's all in good fun but this time it went beyond that. Personally I feel that if you don't want to do an interview, you just tell your PR you don't wanna do them right then. Ever since the South American tour I felt that interviews weren't really doing any good, all people wanted to was bait us, and so I stopped doing 'em, it's that simple."

There was to be a final point of realization for Faith No More, as Bottum explains.
"When it came down to us talking shit about ourselves in the press, that was fine it didn't matter, it didn't bother me. But when it came down to pointing the finger at other people and talking shit about someone else, that's when it bothered me. I think the last Matt Smith Melody Maker article [dated August 8th 1992] was the one that got me, we just sounded like a bunch of idiots. He portrayed us as this band that just talked shit about other people, even if it was Guns N'Roses which may be nearly justified, just to be seen as this band who talks shit about people implies that we think we're better than all these people we're talking shit about. That's really ugly, I mean who are we to be saying that kinda stuff? The responses that article got 'who are this band, who the hell do they think they are?' really bugged me. We got together as a band at that point and said 'look, we talk a lotta shit we've gotta start talking less'. It actually sparked a band meeting.

"When we'd talk about ourselves and give ourselves shit before, it was kinda refreshing in comparison to putting other people down. But then when 'Angel Dust' came out, it was

another confusing record that people couldn't really figure out. So interviews were looked at to explain it, and we talked shit about people, ourselves, in those interviews. Which isn't what that record's about and isn't really what this band's about. People came to talk less and less about the music we were doing and more and more about the people we were being, which was aggravating yes."

Of course, Bottum does concede that the nature of the industry is, for the most part, all about personalities and not about music.
"I think it is unless you're the type of band that talks about the music and what you do seriously, and take yourself very seriously. Unless you're the band that falls into that sort of circus of 'ourselves what we do our music look how fresh exciting and original we are,' unless you play that game, that is the way it's going to happen."

Finally media manipulation had got boring and troublesome for Faith No More.
"We figured we were gonna get manipulated anyway, so we might as well paint the most fabulously grotesque picture we could if only for the personal satisfaction of abusing the media. We used to just 'do it up' to the extreme, and we did that with the Matt Smith piece in late 192. When we saw the piece, we realized things had gotten out of control and that we had to start making sure the band was taken more seriously. We could see the potential problems ahead if we continued on that path."

The band continued touring the US as theatre headliners with Helmet in support, before heading back over to Europe and headlining there with L7 in support. After Christmas, in January 1993, they once again toured the States with Babes In Toyland and Kyuss in support but were bemused to find that 'Angel Dust' had done it's time in the States and that overseas was where Faith No More's immediate future lay. The band were huge in Europe, doubling their 'Real Thing' sales in all European markets. There was a feeling of disappointment that Warner/Reprise didn't make 'Easy' the same smash-hit here as it had been in Europe (it reached number three on the UK charts) but the label reportedly didn't quite know where to push the single. There was still the perception of Faith No More as just a hard rock band, and everyone was afraid to mess with that image. It arguably cost Faith No More a hit, 'Easy' at one point looking like it was going to smash through. But there was no

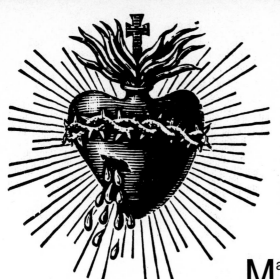

video for MTV to push, and with Europe screaming for the band to return and tour extensively, Faith No More took off for 5 months overseas road-work in March.

Martin's opinions on just about everything continued to differ from the other four. The slow, ugly, bubbling stew of discontent had long been cooking and clues as to it's root are no clearer. Undoubtably Martin's ability to click straight into the atmosphere of the G N'R rock-world, and his comfort generally with being in a major rock band, are factors. There are times when the rest of Faith No More seem almost guilty of their success, guilty of being in the big leagues, as though that nasty underground spectre haunts them once in a while and prays upon their consciences.

MARTIN: "All that stuff is merely self-serving bullshit that doesn't mean anything. There's really no reason to be embarrassed about it or believe it to be true or anything, it's just what's happening there. It's somewhat of an inconvenience in as much as you come out of a hotel and have to sign autographs, but that's about the size of it. I can't really say what the deal is with them on that front."

But somewhere along the line that 'We Care...'/ 'Introduce...' /'Real Thing' camaraderie got lost.

"We've never had much camaraderie, but we were just in situations where we spent a lot of time together. As I said earlier, for me things started to get ugly on the South American tour. At that point I thought everybody was pretty isolated, and any camaraderie was pretty artificial. There's an awful lot of talk and I'm really not sure if there is a problem [now] or not. I personally have a problem. I really didn't like the direction the last record took, the effort that was put into it or the way it went. I don't know what will happen if it goes that way again, time will tell..."

There has long stood the argument that the volatile chemistry that exists serves the band creativity very well. Even that one doesn't cut it anymore.

BOTTUM: "It seems that comes up a lot, people saying 'if you didn't have

"that nasty underground spectre haunts them once in a while and prays upon their consciences.."

that chemistry of wanting to hit each other would you have that special whatever it is you have'. I don't see it contributing to anything, I see it as a downfall. If we're not getting along and if someone else in the band is bugging someone else, I don't see it as a good thing and I don't see it as very helpful at all no. It happens, sure, I look up to my left and see someone [onstage] not getting into the show we're playing, that's aggravating. I've seen people like Jim get into the show in the past, and now he doesn't seem to get into the show in the same way as before and that bothers me. I don't see it ever working for the band, I see it as working against the band."

GOULD: "There have been times, especially on this latest tour, where I've stopped myself whilst playing. I'm hurting myself, slamming into this song and I look across stage and see him twiddling around with his wrist. And it takes me all the strength I have not to pick up a

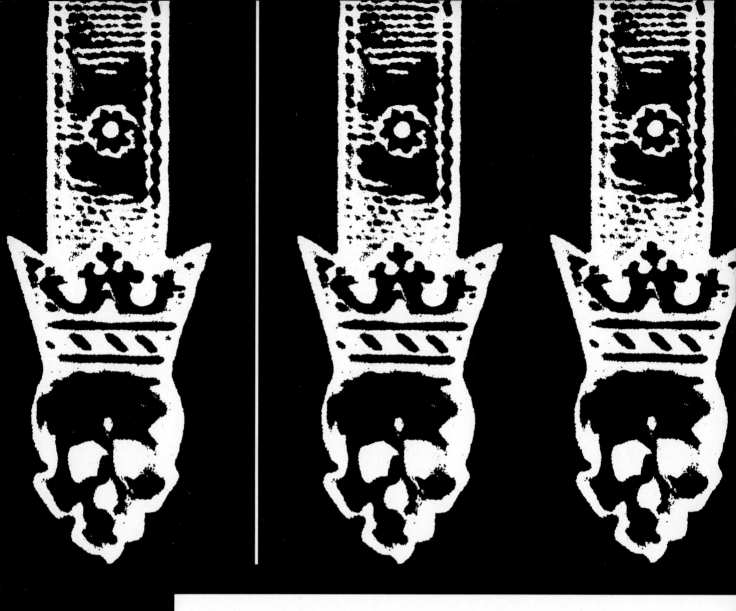

bottle and heave it at him as hard as I can. Those are new feelings."

Faith No More do not change their pants privately. If they need changing they're off whatever and where ever they may be. Patton's only just feeling that he's opened a line of communication with a band that doesn't like to discuss too much.

GOULD: "Everybody's opinion is valid in our democracy, but then when we get to a 'we should talk to him about this' situation it becomes a case of 'what's the point what good will it do?' The irony of everything is that Jim, to this day, will say that open communication with Patton over the Bungle thing didn't work. He'll tell me it didn't do any good. He's not a communicator, he doesn't believe in it."

Is there a hope of saving the situation with Jim?

"We need to sit down and talk. It wouldn't do us any good now because we need to get on with our touring. I know the next record will be a great record, and whatever has to be done will be done to make sure that it is."

What follows, is the full transcript of an interview done with the band members for a Kerrang! magazine article during January 1993. I had initially approached the piece with an idea of interviewing the whole band together. I had mis-calculated the severity of their inharmonious situation. Bordin near enough exploded at the thought, yelling how that

couldn't happen, how it would fuck everything up, how they had a lot of touring left to do. This piece, therefore, is the first one to truly stumble upon the degree of animosity brewing between the band and Jim Martin. It has been purposely left un-edited to illustrate further the growing tensions and frustrations that had been brewing ever since 'Angel Dust's creation. No-one wants to actually say that this line-up may be on it's last tour, but throughout the piece you get the impression this is exactly what is lying in the band's inner-mind. It also deals with Roddy Bottum's revelation of his homosexuality, something which people close to the band had for a long time known but not seen as an issue. Kerrang! magazine had briefly touched on the issue, but finally the NME's Gina Morris had popped the question, got the answers and suddenly everyone wanted a 'Roddy gay' story. He still doesn't fully understand what all the fuss is about: neither do the band.

tick tick tick...Faith No More, the most talented and beautiful time bomb in the history of modern music, are at another of their 'turning points'. 'Angel Dust', whilst not selling as well in the USA as 'The Real Thing', is their most successful album yet in the UK ("Thank goodness for the British!" proclaimed Mike Bordin) and the song that threatens to catapult them to UK chart immortality is one written by a cheesy '70's band called The Commadores who pretty much none of you have heard. Gene Simmons of Kiss recently told Mike Patton (complete with gentle, tender arm squeezes) that he had thought of 'Easy' as a risk. A risk that has seen them at #3 in the charts. And y'know (tick tick tick) this is around the time in months-after-it's- release that 'The Real Thing' bust wide open.

tick tick tick...Never have Faith No More been so close yet so far away. Live shows are top-notch genial affairs, yet a problem exists. And when a Faith No More problem comes to media light, we all tend to laugh it off as a bit of cheap inner-conflict and attempt to goad them into piss-fighting. Not this time. This doesn't have a personality root, it's down to the following: Jim Martin and the other members disagree on key points pertaining to music and writing involvement. The theory that the entire band are working on, is to tour until whenever and get down to repair work in the Autumn. If that is still an option by then. Be aware that this friction isn't a sudden thing, it's been in the air good and strong since the recording of 'Angel Dust'. But no one's interested in open heart surgery right now, indeed Bordin is upset at the thought of a direct five-member confrontation mid-tour. He's afraid it might upset the procarious balance that is currently present. True professionals they've become, Faith No More will simply continue to gel on stage night after night after night as the shit piles under the carpet...

RRRIIIINNNGGG! Wakey wakey rise and shine! Have you all

noticed how much more a part of FNM Mike Patton has become during this album and tour? In the race to exploit every stupid childish act FNM indulge themselves in whilst on tour with the 'big boys', Patton's development from frontman to semi-genius seems to have escaped pens and paper internationally. He has become THE definition for mischievous, curious and warped youths worldwide, a man who will try anything just to try it, who will do anything just to do it. but maybe the biggest 'do it' for Patton was actually becoming a happy member of Faith No More. I ask him when during the album's recording the penny dropped.

"It's pretty simple, at first the fruit wasn't ripe but it's got riper and riper and now it tastes really good. of course the direction of the songs [ie. more extreme] had something to do with it but the actual point at which it clicked is hard to pin down. One thing about this band is there's many things we've either not had the courage or the means to do. But I think we're beginning to care less how it's perceived and just get on with things, just DO THEM."

Its probably easier for him now, looking back, to surmise why he was so antagonistic when he first joined FNM.
"Well, I could have adapted real easily but the truth is I didn't really wanna join, I wanted to know about the band in my own

way. There were certain things I wanted to know and I saw a lot of things I didn't wanna know so I ignored them. Rather than dealing with them and confronting issues I found it much easier to ignore them."

Was becoming the pin-up kid for 1989 the sort of thing we're talking about?

"Yeah definitely, everything, I mean when you're green, hell! I didn't care, I didn't give a shit and if somebody wanted to yank me down the street by my balls then great because I'd never been yanked before."

So the general belligerence and antagonism was just to get through things?

"No, definitely not to get through it. That stuff wasn't for a specific end or reaction, it was just instinct. Even with 'inter-band relationships' it was pure instinct. I mean when you enter a volatile situation anyway, with the thing spiraling towards the toilet, you just stir it a little more. I guess with this album we were all spiraling in the same direction with this album."

Did you find encouragement to express some of your weirder

"I dunno we'd better talk to the psychiatrist..."

and more fucked up ideas, such as the aggressive 'Malpractice' and the twisted 'RV'.

"It's not really aggression more than it's just feeling comfortable being able to unload everything, shit, everything rather than filtering it. There was just a better forum for extremes."

Did you feel that, to a degree, you reinvented yourself with the haircut, the uglier tones, the darker personnas than the smooth white pretty boy of yore? I mean who the hell is the RV pig?

"Haha whadya mean, that's autobiographical...I dunno we'd better talk to the psychiatrist..."

So there was no conscious effort 'fuck this I'll never be a Sassy Magazine pretty boy again'?

"No, nothing conscious and anyway I love Sassy Magazine. Certain things just happen naturally. When you've toured for two years and you're trapped in a time capsule like that you come back fucked up."

was there this bitterness of 'missing your youth'?

"Na, it's just you really get to feel like a rat sometimes because all you can do is run along with it, chasing the trail of cheese. That's all you end up feeling like, in the end you lose dignity you really do. So you end up convincing yourself 'goddamit I have control here' when you obviously don't."

So why is it so much easier now than before?

"I dunno, that's a relationship question. Explaining it would be like

"there's this deep myth about lyricis.."

sitting down with Mom and explaining why you farted at the dinner table three years ago."

How many of the songs you write are based on real-life versus characters you've created?
"I find it hard to create things out of thin air, I can't play Dungeons And Dragons. I need some sort of stimulus, which is bad, but that's the say it is. 'RV' is based on some of my relatives, and everyone has people like that somewhere in their lineage, I mean I'm nothing, I'm no nationality."
Is it therapeutic dealing with characters like that in song form, getting the anger out?
"No because sometimes it isn't a plague, sometimes it isn't a disease and it isn't good to have that shit out in the open off your chest. Why should you show anyone any of that shit," he takes a deep sigh before smirking, "there's this deep myth about lyricists and singers that they're always 'projecting their inner-most secrets' which is horse-shit, totally romantic bullshit. Singers are the WORST! They can't hide behind instruments."

A funny thing happened when I was at the Hollywood Palladium watching Faith fuck with LA's 'hippest coolest' flannel-decked twerpies; I saw Chuck Mosely, the band's ex-singer. He's bigger now, more brutish and sported a shabby beard. He was sweating a lot. 'We Care A Lot' (one of the song's Chuck co-wrote solely with Roddy Bottum) was playing. I asked him how he was and he told me OK except that no-one ever gave him enough fuckin respect and

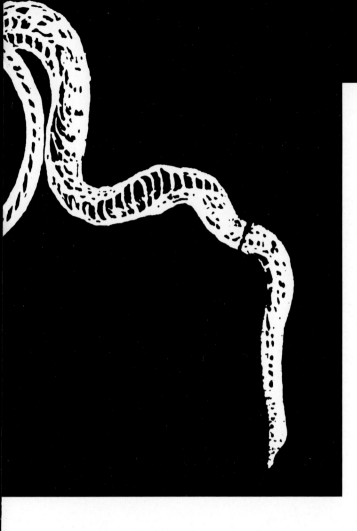

fuck this and fuck that and fuck the other for that matter and did-he-sound-bitter?! Yes, yes Chuck did sound bitter. He's a father now and also has what is said to be a great band called Cement. Yet still he was there, at The Palladium, investing time and energy in torturing himself to a state of malevolent anger. Coulda been him? Maybe. We shall never know because when it counted he wasn't all there...

Mike Bordin is in as constantly intense a state as he's ever been these days. He is maybe sometimes too smart and too bright to deal with problems. Puffy gets flustered easily, and the flustered man tends to go in circles rather than lines, 'how why how can it work'. Billy Gould, meanwhile, remains the Master Of Mischief but in a more clandestine fashion. Along with Puffy, 'tis Gould who carries the weight of Faith No More on his shoulders (by choice no extra cost). Subsequently he isn't quite as ready to dive head-first into humour, but is more content to indulge in a month long game of Dungeons And Dragons on his Macintosh portable lazing in the confines of his bunk. I ask both about whether the problems with

Martin, the faulty engine, can be repaired.
BORDIN: "Sure, anything's possible..."
GOULD: "Stranger things have happened..."
BORDIN: "In another way I don't really know that ANYTHING right now is faulty, because we're playing as well and consistently as ever and that's what matters right now."
Why is the consistency so much greater?
GOULD: "Because we still have the potential to put on great live shows and make great records."
BORDIN: "That's why I think it's a bit of a misnomer to say 'faulty engine'. Which is why YOU have to choose how you frame this whole situation very carefully. yes it DOES matter, yes it IS concerning a lot of things and there's a lot of people who read these things that will really get upset by what YOU say. So YOU have to frame it carefully. All I would say is that we are concerned with getting better, we would be fucked if we didn't try to improve ourselves and the next record will also be an improvement."

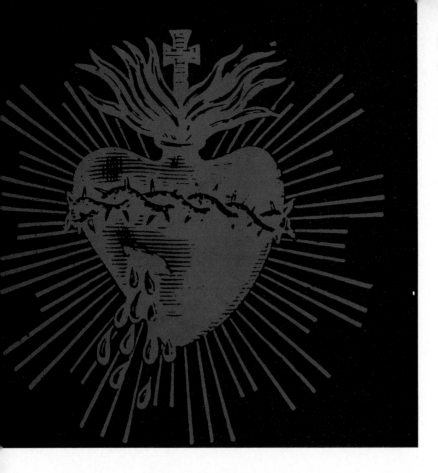

The making of 'Angel Dust' seemed fraught with tension and pressure to follow-up.

"No no," sighs Gould, "we were running parts of the running race with a bum leg! Basically it's like a puzzle, you've got a square peg and a round hole and it isn't fitting and you get frustrated. When you write songs they either work or don't work, if you're a musician and you're writing a song that doesn't work you get frustrated, that's just what you do. We would not have put the record out if it didn't work, but we managed to pull it off, I mean we ended up scrapping lots of songs making sure."

Surely in the old small days artistic freedom was easier because you weren't a 'major' band...

GOULD: "Listen listen listen, as far as the 'artistic freedom' goes and all that bullshit, nobody heard our album until it was finished..."

But isn't there this subconscious pressure telling all concerned 'two million last time two million..'. Didn't someone from your label or somewhere make the statement 'I hope you lot haven't bought houses' after hearing this album for the first time?

"Yeah that's true but it as after the LP was done and anyway, there's always pressure. With 'The Real Thing' we had the pressure of making the record as soon as possible just so as we could get our fucking

"We've *always* had complete artistic freedom and control.."

union scale and pay rent and eat food y'know. There's *always* something, if you have no money it's the money you can get from making an album, if you go on tour there's a per diem everyday, it all becomes the same thing."

BORDIN: "You've missed the point that we made 'The Real Thing' for us, as we wanted and we ended up having a hit with 'Epic' which no-one had really thought of as a 'single' but a lot of people liked as a good song. So we learned that a good song that we like is more than enough. We've *always* had complete artistic freedom and control, we've *never* had anyone telling us what to fucking do. The songwriting has always been US."

Have you been hit with that horrible spiral that asks 'what is a Faith No More song?' and found yourselves trying to write one?

BORDIN: "A Faith No More song is whatever comes out of his ass in the morning, my nose or what he pisses out or he vomits, it's whatever we want."

GOULD: "We've never had that problem, I don't know what a Faith No More song is we just write what we wanna write."

It seems like there's not as much humour or general whackiness evident these days.

BORDIN: "Well I don't know how many shows you've seen but I don't agree at all. If we had a spot in our set where we wrote 'Jizzlobber' 'Woodpecker From Mars'. We could do it like that, but it would be wrong. We still have hilarious funny moments but they don't happen everyday."

"For the past 10 years we've been playing as professionals. We get offered to be on this huge tour, stadiums, and we figure that this is were it all leads to, the highest point.."

GOULD: "For the first few years you put humour first, everything's a big joke and so on. But then you look back and see that the humour is overshadowing other things you realize it can't be that way all the time. There's so many things about this band that have never made it to print or photos, people haven't seen there's a lot of dimensions here. It's easy to talk about what a bunch of smart-asses we are, how our 'funky grooves' or 'metal' there's so many single angles that it can a little tiring."

BORDIN: "We are very focused on making our hour and a half the best we can, in getting the job done properly and in that sense maybe we're the ones who are worse-off. Because we have a standard that we now hold ourselves to and if we don't make that standard we get really pissed off. We're headlining and we've all grown into this sense of responsibility that there *are* people who buy tickets a month in advance, who plan to see our show."

One thing Faith No More haven't outgrown is a good moan. Whilst 'Epic' was breaking them last tour they were whining about 'being successful but not having money yet', seemingly sceptical of their success. This time there was the infamous 'Axl bashing'. I mean, if y'hate it that much then you leave.

GOULD: "To tell you the truth was that it wasn't that bad for the first couple of months, but after four months and being contracted to do it...there were lots of little things. I mean we were treated really well throughout, we can't complain about that at all."

Was it discomfort at being associated with the 'rock circus'?

BORDIN: "If that's what the 'rock circus' was and that's what we saw, then yeah, because that is not something to aspire to. It doesn't seem to me to have anything to do with stretching yourself (creatively)."

GOULD: "For the past 10 years we've been playing as professionals. We get offered to be on this huge tour, stadiums, and we figure that this is were it all leads to, the highest point. But to be on that level you have to *want* to be on that level. Subconsciously you think of things in stages, levels of touring, and you tour at the biggest level and it's a disappointment because you see a lot of unreal things, a lot of bullshit. And whether it's conscious or sub-conscious you wonder to yourself 'is this where I'm headed? Is this where it all leads to? To this bullshit?' But that isn't true. The conditioning of this industry is that that's where you go, to head for that level as opposed to doing something that

you're comfortable and happy with at whatever level. If you headline stadiums you've gotta want to do that, which s great if you're into it, but I think we learnt that we aren't the type of people who could do something like that."

Of course it's to late for all that. The same people who bought 'November Rain' have doubtless bought 'Easy' also and Faith No More left their core audience behind long long ago.

"Which is great," exclaims Bordin, "it comes back down to bringing the same stuff to the table, we still write the way we've always written, we still cover the types of song we'd always cover. As far as 'Easy' is concerned, we were covering that at the same time as 'War Pigs' and before that we did 'Jump'...maybe 'Easy's part of the humour huh?"

Months of hearing screams for 'War Pigs' took their toll and 'Easy's the end result.

"What's more frustrating is that the record company in America doesn't know what to do with 'Easy'," starts Gould, "they said 'how do we take it to alternative radio' - so don't. Then it was 'we don't know how to take it to rock radio' - so don't bother take it to fucking pop radio it's a fucking pop song! 'Uh but you're a Heavy Metal band..."

Too 'pop' sometimes, too 'rock' the other, it's nice to confirm that FNM are doing what

"we will do whatever is possible to insure the highest quality we can.."

they do better than ever-confusing the box-heads that lurk within the bowels of the industry. What ever happened to just listening? Agggh.

"What it comes down to is this. We have an unspoken thing which goes 'we will do whatever is possible to insure the highest quality we can, and we are not afraid to take any direction to make us better. It takes a long time to have a relationship with people that know and understand your band. I mean you look at people like Frank Zappa and Neil Young, who are well-respected and that's the sort of band we wanna be, the type that will do whatever is necessary to do it right."

"You're using a lot of phrases that don't apply to us," affirms Bordin, "I mean how would we sell-out right now? Would we have gotten tattoos or fringed jackets? If we were to 'sell-out' and dress funny or try to re-write 'Epic' or 'We Care A Lot' those would be the death of the band. It couldn't happen, we'd hate each other and ourselves."

Interesting to note that, apart from the Martin versus 4 situation, you're all getting along better than ever before whilst also leading more separate lives. But I have to ask, could the Jim situation turn into another 'Chuck Mosely nightmare'?

GOULD: "All I'm saying is that some of the things we went through on the last record we will

not go through again. We made a good record in spite of all the stuff that was going on..."
BORDIN: " I'm tremendously proud of 'Angel Dust', and if that stuff hadn't been going on who knows how much better it may have been."
It's shaping up to be a long hot Autumn with plenty of repairs.
GOULD: "I wanna move on sure..."
BORDIN: "I love my car, of course I do, I wanna fix it up and make it great. There's no question about it."

Roddy Bottum seems more relaxed than ever, a serene figure in a sea of ever-evolving under-currents and madness. He has found ways of releasing the tensions through a combination of outrageous fashion and open discussion on his being gay.
"I cannot believe people didn't know sooner, to me it was always pretty obvious in the videos where I've been this typically obvious homosexual figure. Between being the 'cowboy', the 'cop', even in bondage, it's always been out in the open. And there's no real reason or motive for me coming out and saying I'm gay now, there's no real political agenda or anything, it just felt right finally. Of course I sympathize with gay rights, but I'm not talking about being gay so as I can become like this 'rock spokesperson' on homosexuality. I'd never been asked before [the NME interview] and I decided to talk about it because I was asked. I mean to me, it really isn't a big deal. The symbolism's been there and people haven't picked up on it and that's fine, that's OK, it's not important that they do or don't."

"I don't think people see us as being intelligent and sarcastic.."

"I think it was everybody's job on this last album to stretch, for everyone to take a step forward. I don't see anything I'm doing now as being any greater or more than before, but of course I had to come out and forward even more which is something you take for granted. We have to do that with every album."
Indeed, 'tis Rod that puts the POP into Faith No More.
"That's the stuff I listen to more than anyone else in the band.'
Bottum is the POP and Martin is the metal. Two extremes that have co-habited with superb results. Until now? I ask Bottum for his view on what is a disturbing rift.
"Jim and I are absolute extremes and the balance will always be there, but to enable the scales to keep balance the further I go in my direction the further he has to go in his. If he stays where he stays and I continue to go further, then things will go off-kilter. I would hope that he would next time come up with even bigger riffs. On the last album I didn't see him

moving so much in his direction, he kinda stayed where he was and not only that he didn't produce a whole lot of material. So as it stands right now it is a little off kilter, but we'll just have to work it out. The outcome depends on so many things, we can repair things but..." he's lost for words on the issue, scrambling for the right combination. They won't come out. We move a little further on.

Opposites being what they are, Roddy has a quite different view of the current live shows to Martin (as you'll read later).
"I'm extremely happy with the shows, they're more in a a direction than I thought they'd be, there's more aggression than ever before too. Mike Patton's performance has improved so much, and the intensity level has upped to a point where we take it much more seriously."
Have Faith No More grown from boys to men?
"I suppose that's somewhat accurate. I mean our initial success with 'the Real Thing' was so unexpected that you kinda have to go HA HA
and laugh at it, laughing at everything's your only guard. And you can only do that so long before you start looking like an idiot. We did it for a long time, we laughed at our success and then we realized that by laughing at our success we were laughing at all the people who'd bought our records. When we started to realize that, things had to change..."
Was there intense embarrassment that, to Dave in Iowa, 2 million albums puts you in the same basket as (BLLEEUURRGGHH) Great White or whatever?
"Almost embarrassing yeah, it's your biggest hope and also your biggest expectation and fear, all of them. Suddenly you're not as 'underground' anymore so you lose there, you've sold a lot of records so Dave in Iowa is listening to you and you're not what you used to be, this 'cherished thing' for the 'in' few, you're this big exposed band. More than embarrassment and discomfort, I think it just took some adjusting to."

"I mean our initial success with 'the Real Thing' was so unexpected that you kinda have to go HA HA.."

Adjustments which still haven't quite kicked in. Moaning on 'The Real Thing' about this and that, the rigours of fame (sob) and NOW whinging about playing to 40,000 people a night? I thought you'd learnt that lesson once. Why didn't you just leave if it was so ugly?
"I guess it was discomfort again. We weren't into that whole scene, it wasn't what we were about but you're right, we were stupid and we should've just split. Would've been the gentle-

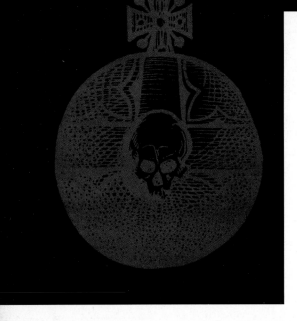

manly thing to do."

Are you an easy target for us? We can see you're easy to wind-up.

"I don't think people see us as being intelligent and sarcastic when they do that, they see us more as being stupid and idiots who will say anything and put their feet in their mouths. If i was a journalist and I saw what we'd said in print, I'd probably assume we were idiots."

Are the doors closing on Goofyville Gossip land?

"Pretty much, and I think it all comes down to one conversation we had a while ago. It's stupid to complain about who we hate all the time to the press, plus I'm pretty much bored of it. But when you're asked that 10 millionth time about Axl Rose you just think who cares."

And then for him to be upset enough to slap your wrists personally?

"That was really humiliating that whole thing, *that* made us think too. I don't know the guy that well but he seemed genuinely hurt, just this honest guy saying 'hey there's only two bands I really like and I took one of them out with me which is you guys and then you bad-mouth me in the press. They did us a huge favour and then for us to turn around and say that stuff in the press was pretty shitty."

"it was a case of going in the absolute furthest opposite direction.."

The pop sensibilities combined with the intense sarcasm is what ended up producing a #3 cover-hit. Pop-Bottum's the one to explain why.

"The motivation was kinda to fuck with people," laughs Roddy, "we'd been covering this the same time as 'War Pigs' and kids would literally expect us to do 'War Pigs'. So being the assholes we are, we hear people screaming for 'War Pigs' it was a case of going in the absolute furthest opposite direction. I mean, if we hear people shout for something that hard, we aren't going to give it to them. 'Easy' was the cheesiest pop song we could think of, in America it was a staple of the '70's here wheras in he UK it isn't as well known. Why is it doing so well over there?

Jim Martin sits, as ever, like an old man. He fiddles and tweaks with a scanner, prying into other people's affairs as the bus steams for Santa Barbara.

"Hey...wait a minute. It's yer old lady and she's got a guy in the house and they're...oooh ooooh HAHAHAHA..."

He has become an aural voyeur, hoping to catch a wild sex-phone thing or at the very least a decent argument. It's perhaps the most convincing argument yet that cellular phones shouldn't be used for important calls because it isn't long before this man links up scanner with tape recorder.

Cagey, a touch aggravated, I ask Martin about 'Easy', a song he doesn't like.

"Yeah, never really did like the song, I mean it's OK I guess. I didn't even wanna record it but we elected to do so, but I suppose (laughs) as far as it being the biggest song about-to-be-added-to-our-LP (laughs again) CD's, tapes to the best of my knowledge that's what's gonna happen."

It's maybe down to the combination of people. This is the thing, as a unit you may have chemistry but individually you may have fuck all. Maybe a band who loses a member would be doomed."

After all these months on tour, he can still get his jollies off onstage?

"Hmmm...infrequently it has to be said," replies the behemoth honestly enough, "maybe once a week."

Is it just the monotony of touring, or are we back to the 'it' factor that's going to need fixing?

"We're back to the 'it' factor. Hopefully when we do the next record we can work 'it' out and get on track."

I put it to Martin that this is more serious than the usual whacky-black FNM humour.

"I dunno...I don't know what 'it' is. I mean I can speculate as to what 'it' is but there's nothing that can be nailed down as such."

In a sense Martin's just as reluctant to get involved in piss-fighting as the other four band members, choosing instead a passage of verbal mirrors to bounce off the obvious point: that he is currently an unpopular FNM'er who doesn't want to confront the issues head-on anymore than anyone else. I put it to Martin that he *seems* disconnected from the rest of the band; he's in the back lounge they're in the front. He doesn't know how they really feel, he is left speculating. No camaraderie in the workplace. Those have to be hard working conditions.

"The best thing to do is to look at things with your own two eyes. I look at things with mine and make the best sense of what I see."

It seems as if, on stage at least, the band are doing their best shows ever.

"Well that's for someone who's outfront to say, to me onstage it doesn't always seem that way, it seemed that there was maybe more raw energy comin' off the stage in the past. But y'see that's for me, for Mike Patton there's probably a lot more energy than ever before..."

Well when you stand and look at them...

"Look at who?"

The rest of the band.

"I really don't tend to look at them that much y'know."

Isn't there this delicate chemistry' that requires interaction to make things what they are?

"Probably but it's nothing we know anything about, it's maybe down to the combination of people. This is the thing, as a unit you may have chemistry but individually you may have fuck all. Maybe a band who loses a member would be doomed."

AUTHOR'S INTERLUDE #5

It is July 4th 1993, two weeks before Faith No More end their 'Angel Dust' World Tour. Onstage, at a Belgian festival called Werchter in front of 60,000 people, the delicacies of the Martin versus band situation are making themselves even clearer. Gould is pretty much at his wit's end, summoning all powers of self-control to avoid exploding in frustrated rage. Patton, too, has plainly had enough. Bordin is concerned, worried, as always analytical about the situation. As much as he and Jim don't see eye to eye, they have known each other far too long for Bordin to feel vindictive. And Roddy Bottum appears distraught, worried, racked with guilt. He talks of feeling bad that this whole issue hasn't been discussed and sorted out long ago, that everyone's trying to get through this extremely trying spell without tackling the head-on.

Martin is in a quiet state of denial. It's a painful thing to watch, the Big Sick Ugly monolith now generally quiet and solitary. Things have gone too far, he surely knows that, yet it is too much for him to step forward and make the first (conciliatary) move for the good of the long-term picture. Perhaps because that long-term picture involves music that will, doubtless, be more like 'Angel Dust' s progressive direction than anything else. And Jim Martin has made it clear all along that he feels 'Angel Dust' was sub-par, a poor effort that could've been bettered.

The saddest aspect of the rift is that Martin has shut himself off from one of the band's premier strengths, their thirst for absorbing musical extremes and opposites. Martin talks of 'having to write especially for Faith No More', whilst the band want his wildest, most twisted metal nightmares. Communication breakdown? There was never any to fail in the first place.

The strangest thing is how little this crisis affects the band's live performance. In Werchter, they put on one of their most scintillating hows of the whole tour, fraught with tension and crackling with strong energies, a 5 piece fight just begging to go off. Patton takes off around the stage with his dick hanging out after the crowd have sung the chorus to 'Midlife Crisis' (t'was an affectionate gesture). He later hurls himself repeatedly into the stage, continuing

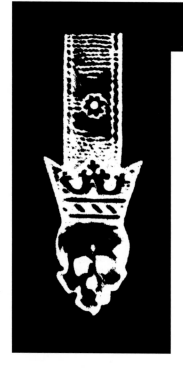

his love affair with masochistic self abuse. Then, with his back to the stage, Patton instinctively hurls a bottle of water over his shoulder towards Martin...it misses by two feet. Had it been a strike, that *surely* would have been the catalyst necessary to bring this whole thing boiling over. Before the show, everyone agrees that it's in the band's best interests to try and cancel the two weeks in South America. The band enjoy touring there, Gould and Patton especially enjoying the cultural diversities and color of the continent, but there is the growing feeling that the ugly, cancerous problem should be taken care of as soon as possible. It's been unhealthy for long enough, and everyone has reached the limit of their tolerance.

Both Gould and Bordin are excited about the future, each talking about starting the writing process for the next album within 3 weeks of being back at home. Patton will get the break his shin-splints demand, and he's already bubbling with enthusiasm. As is Bottum. Which all leaves the Martin situation a forgone conclusion; he's out! Right? Wrong.

GOULD: "Whatever happens you have to remember this, and this is the most important thing. That we've had a lot of good times with Jim and you can't just say 'fuck this fuck that fuck him,' because it isn't nearly that simple. All we want to do is find a situation that works."

Martin feels there could be so much more if Faith No More want to take it.

"I still don't feel we've achieved 'that' success. It doesn't even feel lucky to have sold 2.5 million albums or whatever, I believe there's more to come if we wanna go for it. We've reached a certain level using a certain method. We've made ourselves known right? So now, we don't have to do all that smart-ass shit-talkin' stuff anymore. Unless we just want to. I don't think there's really anything to be gained from it at this point, because lots of people are now paying attention to us whether they like us or not."

Matt Wallace is convinced that the future of Faith No More is something they control exclusively.

"I think if any member of the band decide something is worthwhile and want to pursue it, then they'll do it. As long as you have a core of three who have made a decision, then it'll happen. As far as Jim is concerned I don't know what the final outcome will be, there were a lot of grumbles in the studio but I don't know too much since. I do think if Faith No More want to change members every couple of album, they could continue to exist. It'd become this evolving amoeba-type thing, and it wouldn't be the Faith No More of 'The Real Thing' but it would always evolve. As long as there's 3 guys who want to pursue Faith No More in any situation, and they wanna find people to augment it, they can survive."

For now, despite the severity of the emotions involved, the door remains ever-so-slightly ajar. One thing is certain though. That whatever happens, Faith No More will always remain a creative time-bomb. A band held together by a core of genial talent. And the stubborn refusal to pack up and walk away quietly...

THE END.

134

FAITH NO MORE - DISCOGRAPHY

Albums

14th Sept 1987	Introduce Yourself	LP	SLAP 21	Faster Disco	We Care A Lot
		CD	8280512	Anne's Song	R'N'R
		MC	SMAC 21	Introduce Yourself	The Crab Song
				Chinese Arithmetic	Blood
				Death March	Spirit
3rd July 1989	The Real Thing	LP	828154.1	From Out Of Nowhere	The Real Thing
		CD	828154.2	Epic	Underwater Love
		MC	828154.4	Falling To Pieces	The Morning After
				Surprise! You're Dead!	Woodpecker From Mars
				Zombies Eaters	
				Additional tracks on CD/MC	Edge Of The World
					War Pigs
16th July 1990	The Real Thing Limited Edition Picture Disc	LP	828217.1	As 'The Real Thing', 828154.1	
4th February 1991	Live At Brixton	LP	828238.1	Falling To Pieces	From Out Of Nowhere
		CD	828238.2	The Real Thing	We Care A Lot
		MC	828238.4	Epic (Pump Up The Jam)	Zombie Eaters
				War Pigs	Edge Of The World
				Additional tracks on CD/MC	The Grade
					The Cowboy Song
8th June 1992	Angel Dust	LP	828321.1	Land Of Sunshine	Kindergarten
		CD	828321.2	Caffeine	Be Agressive
		MC	828238.4	Midlife Crisis	A Small Victory
				R.V.	Jizzlobber
				Everything's Ruined	Smaller & Smaller
				Malpractice	
				Additional tracks on CD/MC	Crack Hitler
					Midnight Cowboy
24th August 1992	Angel Dust (With Interview CD)	CD	828326.2	As 'Angel Dust' with free interview CD	
29th January 1993	Angel Dust (With Easy)	CD	828401.2	As 'Angel Dust' with 'Easy'	
		MC	828401.4		

Singles

18th January 1988   **We Care A Lot**

7"	LASH 17	a: We Care A Lot	b: Spirit
12"	LASHX 17	a: We Care A Lot	b1: Spirit
			b2: Chinese Arithmatic (Radio Mix)

18th April 1988   **Anne's Song**

7"	LASH 18	a: Anne's Song (Remix)	b: Greed
12"	LASHX 18	a: Annes's Song (Dance Mix)	b: Greed
7" Picture Disc	LASHP 18	a: Anne's Song (Remix)	b: Greed

30th October 1989   **From Out Of Nowhere**

7"	LASH 19	a: From Out Of Nowhere	b: Cowboy Song
12"	LASHX 19	a: From Out Of Nowhere	b1: Cowboy Song
			b2: The Grade

29th January 1990   **Epic**

7"	LASH 21	a: Epic	b: War Pigs (Live)
12"	LASHX 21	a: Epic	b1: War Pigs (Live)
			b2: Surprise You're Dead (Live)
			b3: Chinese Arithmatic (Live)
CD	LASCD 21	1: Epic	3: Surprise You're Dead (Live)
		2: War Pigs (Live)	4: Chinese Arithmatic (Live)
7" Gatefold	LASHG 21	a: Epic	b1: War Pigs (Live)
			b2: Surpirse You're Dead (Live)
7" shaped disc	LASPD 21	a: Epic	b: War Pigs (Live)

2nd April 1990   **From Out Of Nowhere**

7"	LASH 24	a: From Out Of Nowhere	b: Woodpecker From Mars (Live)
12"	LASHX 24	a1: From Out Of Nowhere	b1: The Real Thing (Live)
		a2: Woodpecker From Mars (Live)	b2: Epic (Live)
CD	LASCD 24	1: From Out Of Nowhere	3: The Real Thing (Live)
		2: Woodpecker From Mars (Live)	4: Epic (Live)
Cassette	LASCS 24	1: From Out Of Nowhere	Repeat side 2
		2: Woodpecker From Mars (Live)	
7" Gatefold	LASHG 24	a: From Out Of Nowhere	b1: Woodpecker From Mars (Live)
			b2: Epic (Live)
12" Picture Disc	LASPX 24	a1: From Out Of Nowhere (Extended)	b1: The Real Thing (Live)
		a2: Woodpecker From Mars (Live)	b2: Epic (Live)

FAITH NO MORE - DISCOGRAPHY

2nd July 1990 — **Falling To Pieces**

12"	LASHX 25	a1: Falling To Pieces	b1: Underwater Love (Live)
		a2: We Care A Lot (Live)	b2: From Out Of Nowhere (Live)
Cassette	LASCS 25	1: Falling To Pieces	Repeat side 2
		2: We Care A Lot (Live)	
		3: Underwater Love (Live)	
12" With Poster	LASPX 25	a1: Falling To Pieces	b1: Underwater Love (Live)
		a2: We Care A Lot (Live)	b2: From Out Of Nowhere (Live)
7" Gatefold	LASHG 25	a: Falling To Pieces	b1: We Care A Lot (Live)
			b2: Underwater Love (Live)
7" with free patch	LASHP 25	a: Falling To Pieces	b: We Care A Lot (Live)

27th August 1990 — **Epic**

7"	LASH 26	a: Epic	b1: Falling To Pieces (Live At Brixton)
			b2: Epic (Live At Brixton)
Cassette	LASCS 26	1: Epic	Repeat side 2
		2: Falling To Pieces (Live At Brixton)	
		3: Epic (Live At Brixton)	
12"	LASHX 26	a1: Epic	b1: Epic (Live At Brixton)
		a2: Falling To Pieces (Live At Brixton)	b2: As The Worm Turns (Live At Brixton)
CD	LASCD 26	1: Epic	3: Epic (Live At Brixton)
		2: Falling To Pieces	4: As The Worm Turns (Live At Brixton)
7" shaped picture disc	LASPD 26	a: Epic	b: Falling To Pieces (Live At Brixton)

26th May 1992 — **Midlife Crisis**

7" coloured vinyl	LASH 37	a: Midlife Crisis	b1: Jizzlobber
			b2: Crack Hitler
Cassette in box	LASCS 37	1: Midlife Crisis	Repeat side 2
		2: Jizzlobber	
		3: Crack Hitler	
CD picture disc	LASCD 37	1: Midlife Crisis	3: Crack Hitler
		2: Jizzlobber	4: Midlife Cowboy
12" picture disc	LASHX 37	a1: Midlife Crisis	b1: Crack Hitler
		a2: Jizzlobber	b2: Midlife Cowboy

FAITH NO MORE - DISCOGRAPHY

3rd August 1992   A Small Victrory

7" coloured vinyl	LASH 39	a: A Small Victory (Edit)	b: Let's Lynch The Landlord
Cassette in Box	LASCS 39	1: A Small Victory (Edit)	Repeat side 2
		2: Let's Lynch The Landlord	
12" picture disc	LASHX 39	a: A Small Victory	b1: Let's Lynch The Landlord
			b2: Malpractice
CD picture disc	LASCD 39	1: A Small Victory	3: Let's Lynch The Landlord
		2: A Small Victory (Edit)	4: Malpractice

1st September 1992   A Small Victory (Remix)

12"	LASHX 40	a: A Small Victory (R-Evolution 23 (Full Moon) Mix)	b1: A Small Victory (Sundown Mix)
			b2: A Small Victory (Sundown
Instrumental Mix)			
CD	LASCD 40	1: A Small Victory (Youth Remix) Edit	3: A Small Victory (Sundown Mix)
		2: A Small Victory (R-Evolution 23 (Full Moon) Mix)	4: A Small Victory (Sundown
Instrumental Mix)			

9th November 1992   Everything's Ruined

7" coloured vinyl	LASH 43	a: Everythings Ruined (Edit)	b: Midlife Crisis (Live)
Cassette	LASCS 43	1: Everythings Ruined (Edit)	Repeat side 2
		2: Midlife Crisis (Live)	
CD in Wallet	LASCD 39	1: Everythings Ruined (Edit)	3: Land Of Sunshine (Live)
		2: Midlife Crisis (Live)	
CD in Digipack	LACDP 43	1: Everythings Ruined (Edit)	3: R.V. (Live)
		2: Edge Of The World (Live)	

29th December 1992   I'm Easy

7"	LASH 44	a: I'm Easy	b: Be Agressive
Cassette	LASCS 44	1: I'm Easy	Repeat side 2
		2: Be Agressive	
CD in Wallet	LASCD 44	1: I'm Easy	3: A Small Victory
		2: Be Agressive	4: We Care A Lot (Live)
CD in Digipack	LACDP 43	1: Everythings Ruined (Edit)	3: R.V. (Live)
		2: Edge Of The World (Live)	

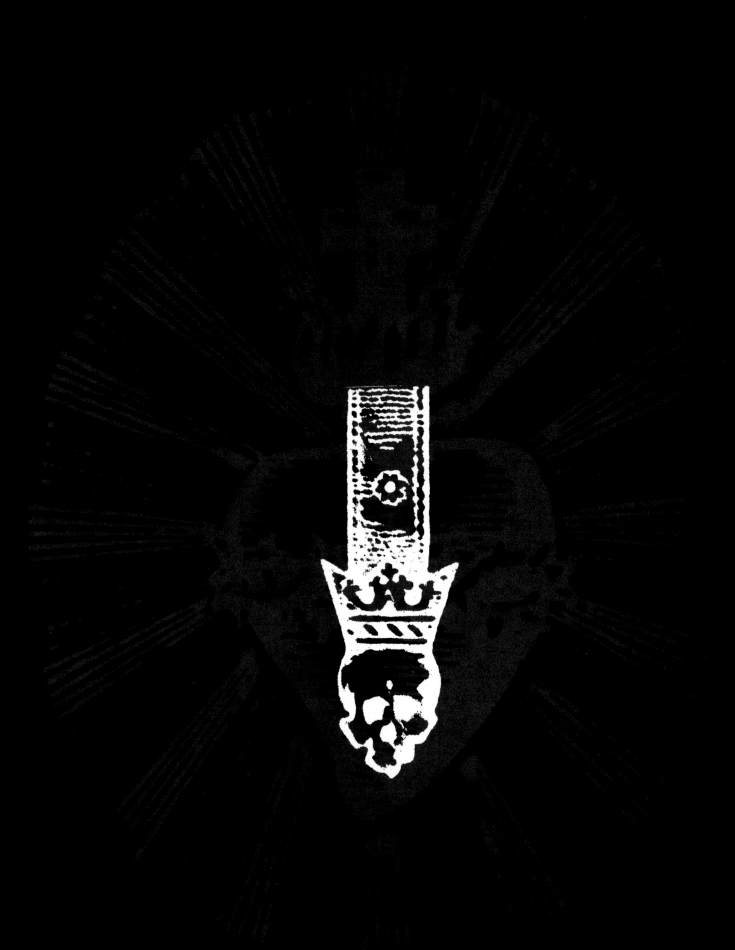

STOP PRESS

December 14th 1993

The long hot Summer wore on and on and on, the dispute between the band and Martin obviously getting no nearer to being resolved. Communications became terse at best, messages being exchanged via fax, and rehearsals were apparently not especially productive. The last third of this book dealt with the very distinct reality that Faith No More would be unable to retain it's current shape, and throughout the history of Faith No More as detailed by those involved, 'love' was never a strong binding factor. On Tuesday November 30th 1993, Jim Martin was sent a band fax, culminating in the decision that their working relationship was terminated.

At the time of writing there are still many legal and financial issues to be resolved, and anyway, as both parties have said, the root of the problems have been extensively discussed elsewhere in this book. It is all quite simple. It all came down to the ever widening gap between Jim Martin and the other four band members as people who could relate to each other in a creative environment. Indeed, most bands would've sorted the whole stinking mess out months before, but the infamous communication problems between band members meant this fight had to go the stubborn, silent distance.

The band are starting to actively seek out a new guitar player, Gould filling in the guitar parts on current demoed ideas in his home studio. During the band's recorded collaboration with Boo-Yaa-Tribe for the 'Judgement Night' soundtrack 'Another Body Murdered', it was Gould who played all guitar parts. And the split may yet work out better for all concerned in terms of better fulfilment and achievement. The band will be free to pursue an avenue obviously not as comfortably open with Martin as a collaborator, whilst he can go on and make the music he really wants to as his own entity. Indeed, one major label is already sniffing the Martin solo trail.
The final words go to Gould and Martin.

BILL

"We have definitely parted company. I think anybody who's read the music press over the past year, even two years, shouldn't be too surprised with what's happened. The situation just came to a point where it was impossible to work together, and we wish Jim all the luck in the world with whatever he does; but we don't plan on working with him any time soon.

"The way the music press works, which is the way mass communication works, is that media is transferred in very simple images. So I think a lot of the preconceptions people have of this band are not entirely accurate in the real sense. Historically Jim has had actually very little to do with most of the songwriting we do. So I think it's the best for both sides really. I think he's talented in his own right and that he should do what he wants to do and what he's good at. I think that what we do has nothing to do with what he does.

"Anything negative I have to say about Jim I've already said in the press whilst he was in the band so I don't see any point in reiterating it. I can't see anything constructive coming out of badmouthing Jim at this point in time! I understand that people will be egging us on (to do so) and that's fine. I love to hear dirt too. I just think that at this point in time it wouldn't do us any good, and my obligations are to this group and making it work. I think we just wanna write a good record. And now circumstances have finally happened that can allow us to write a great record. We're really excited with our new possibilities.

"Hopefully this will be the first terminated relationship that we can work out as human beings, I don't know if we can handle it or not but we'll give it a shot. All I can say is that (throughout) we were really unhappy with the problem and the situation was really bad, but at the same time we were stuck in a situation where we had to work and couldn't dwell upon it. Sometimes when you read things in the music press that you're trying to ignore just because you're trying to get your work done, it turns up the internal pressure and starts getting into paranoia. Probably Jim had a lot of paranoia on his side because he's reading things over which we have no control. But we're dissatisfied and it's in the back of our minds.

"We're writing an awesome record and it's nearly written. In some ways it won't be as drastically different as people probably expect. The songwriting process on this record is the same as it has been throughout. The difference is that we're looking to strip some fat, get some nice, short, to-the-point songs. Coming off touring the last album for a year and a half, which we liked a lot, we felt the need for quick, to-the-point songs. Which is what we're doing. It'll be a little more immediate. And it's our priority to make the best album we can, and be as efficient as possible.

"Anyone who thinks that when changing a person, or by a person looking different, your 'rock' quota will be affected is being very superficial. Anybody who judges the music they listen to by what the bands playing look like, should really re-evaluate why they're spending their money on records and should go and buy fashion magazines instead. Musically, I think the only thing that will change is that we'll get better."

JIM MARTIN

"Faith No More, as you know it, is no longer. I believe the fact that we (always) went in different ways musically was actually an integral part of the band. I am still writing songs, working on music as I have been throughout most of my life, and will continue to do so. Hopefully, I will see you all soon."

To be continued...

PHOTOGRAPHS ARE PRODUCED COURTESY OF :-

IDOLS LICENSING & PUBLICITY
PETE CRONIN
LONDON FEATURES INTERNATIONAL
RELAY PHOTOS
RETNA PICTURES LTD
©1994